Another Lifetime

Felicity Keats et al

Text © Felicity Keats Morrison, Mary Hall, Gwynyth Johnson,
Sandi Koenig 2023
Cover ©Thariq Kader 2023
Editor Sandi Koenig
First Edition 2023

No part of this publication
may be reproduced, stored in a
retrieval system, or transmitted in any form
or by any means, including photocopying,
without written permission
of the publishers.

umSinsi Press
PO Box 28129
Malvern
4055
Kwa-Zulu Natal
South Africa
www.dancingpencils.co.za

ISBN 978-1-4309-0612-4

This memoir is original and all views expressed in the book reflect the author's beliefs. The opinions and views expressed are not those of **umSinsi Press**. We are an independent publishing company whose sacred objective is to provide budding authors with a platform from which their voices can be heard. We believe in publishing information and view-points of different cultures and from different perspectives, in fairness and recognition of our country's wonderful diversity.

Dedication

This book is dedicated to the three wonderful people who helped to create it with their input and expertise. They are

Mary MacLeod Hall, from Scotland, my cousin

Gwynyth Wendy Johnson, from Australia, my sister

Sandi Koenig, from Ballito KwaZulu Natal, my second cousin.

Thank you all so much for your time, enthusiasm and input in helping to give birth to this book.

Contents

Dedication 3
Foreword 1
Acknowledgements 2
Author profile 5
    Felicity Keats Morrison 5
Author profile 10
    Mary MacLeod Hall 10
Author profile 12
    Gwynyth Wendy Johnson 12
Author profile 13
    Sandra (Sandi) Lynn Koenig 13
Another Lifetime 26
    Felicity Keats 26
Family Tree Of People Involved In This Book 30
Chapter 1 32
    Introducing Mary Ann Cole 32
    Introducing John Frederick Baumann 33
    Mary Ann's Pregnancies 38
    John and Fredrick – off to the Goldfields 39
    Mary Ann stranded in Singapore 42
    Mary Ann in Hong Kong 43
    Mary Ann back in England 46

Introducing Florence 47
Chapter 2 49
Florence In Byrne 49
    Introducing Ellen and George More McLeod 49
'Our' MacLeod History Written By Mary MacLeod (Florence's Granddaughter) 50
Connection With Scotland 51
We Don't Know Where We Came From! 55
Some Background History 57
    Jacobite Rebellions 57
Cristall Family 62
    Dictionary of National Biography 63
    The Wreck of the Minerva 64
Florence and Herbert move from Byrne Valley 76
Chapter 3 78
Florence's Children 78
Chapter 4 80
Florence's Children 80
Leytonstone : Harrison Old Main Line, Natal 89
    "Down Memory Lane" 89
    by Richard Herbert Orbin May 1995 89
Zephyr Ridge : Hammarsdale "New" Main Line, Natal 91

Chapter 5 95
   Florence's Children 95
      Hector Percy McLeod (1901 – 1984) 95

Chapter 6 109
   Florence's Children 109
   Constance Ivy MacLeod 109
      Constance (Connie) Ivy McLeod/MacLeod (1904 – 1995) 109

Chapter 7 117
   Florence's Children 117
      More On Constance Ivy MacLeod 117

Chapter 8 130
   Florence's Children 130
      Vera Edna Lloyd (1907 - 1975) 130
      Vera (my mother) 130

Chapter 9 145
   Florence's Grandchildren 145
      Gwynyth Wendy Johnson 145
      (Nee Lloyd) Written By Gwynyth 145

Chapter 10 155
   Florence's Grandchildren 155
      Michael Andrew Lloyd (1935 – 2022) 155

Chapter 11 158

Florence's Grandchildren 158
 Felicity Anne Morrison 158
Section 2 174
Chapter 12 174
 The Byrne Valley 174
  Written by Donald McLeod in 2004 174
Chapter 13 179
 Lily Glen – Jack and Luly Fayers 179
  Written by Felicity Keats 179
More recent family pictures 189
Chapter 14 193
 Blarney 193
  Written by Felicity Keats 193
 Walk from Blarney to Rose Cottage 194
  Mary Macleod Hall Remembers It As Follows: 197
Chapter 15 204
 Blarney 204
  Written By Donald McLeod 204
Chapter 16 219
 Blarney Farm 219
  Written By Donald McLeod 219
 Blarney - Grandpa Fred 221
Chapter 17 229

Donald McLeod's Life at Blarney 229
   Written By Donald McLeod 229
Section 3 244
Chapter 19 244
   The Lloyds 244
      Written By Gwynyth Lloyd Johnson, Sister Of Felicity Lloyd 244
      The Ancestry of Catharina Elizabeth de Waal 1790 - 1863 257
      Authors Note (Gwynyth Lloyd) 259
Chapter 20 260
   Our Immigrant Ancestors 260
   Appendices 273

Foreword

How did this book begin? Just the germ of a suggestion was the start of this book. My daughter Lel, (Lesley Anne Chorn) asked me to write down slivers of what I could remember during my childhood and growing up years. I lay in bed in the predawn hours with one cat sleeping on me and another sleeping next to me and wondered how to do this.

I decided to start with my great great grandmother on my mothers' side, then write about my great grandmother, my grandmother, my mother and her sisters and brother, all of whom I had known, and then write about my mother and father and their three children. All these people deserved a portion of a family tree so you can understand how they all related to one another, being mentioned in this book.

I decided not to go into my adult years so my own children, my grandchildren and nieces and nephews are not part of this story, except for Sandi Koenig. Sandi is my cousin Richard Orbin's daughter and as he is not around to tell his part of the story, Sandi has stood in and is doing a wonderful job.

After writing about my family, I decided to write a small section about the Byrne Valley which was important in the lives of the McLeod's, and as holidays my brother and I had there as children. This is in the second section of the book, and the last section is a history of my father's side, written by my sister Gwynyth Johnson. My father was a descendant of the 1820 settlers in East London. I never had the pleasure of meeting any of them but my sister, who has done extensive research into family history, will tell this story.

Acknowledgements

Now that you know that this is my story and how the story began, I would like to acknowledge help from the following people.

Hilton Keats, my son ... who said to me, please pretty please, retire from business. I will look after your needs. So I did, and gave up running my publishing company, UmSinsi Press cc and also being in charge of the non-profit company, Dancing Pencils Literacy Development Project. Although I stayed in an oversight capacity with both of these, the running of them I delegated into the competent hands of my partner Ayanda Hlabisa, who has been working with me for almost six years and I thank him for competently looking after them both.

This has freed me to spend time looking at the birds, feeding them, and enjoying the many cats that are here. I spend time gazing at the skies which is very liberating and does a lot to help with creativity and this year I have written three adult novels under a nom de plume, one book on literacy development, a recipe book, this book and a new adult novel is also in the process of creation ... so thank you Hilton and Yvette your caring wife.

Mary MacLeod Hall, my cousin in Scotland who has been to visit me and has visited Byrne, Blarney and Rose Cottage where her grandmother lived. Although Mary was born in England and lives in Scotland, Mary is very connected with the MacLeod family, on both her mother and her father's side. On her only visit to me, now twenty eight years ago, Mary spent a perhaps uncomfortable weekend with a group of us in Blind Bentley's cottage on the Blarney farm, just to get a feel of what it was like for those early pioneer settlers. Mary has huge documents with exact dates to help develop this biography of early ancestors which make for a fascinating story that I am sure you will enjoy. She was excited and willingly helped grow this book.

Gwynyth Johnson, my sister, who lives in Australia … Gwyn has been deeply involved in recording genealogy and has documented family history in Wikitree….. and has sent beautiful work on immigrant connections as well as writing the section on the Lloyd side of our family. Gwyn also assisted immensely with the editing.

Lesley Ann Chorn, my daughter, for proof reading and sending us her valuable suggestions.

Sandi Koenig, my second cousin (her father Richard was my dearly beloved cousin) who unearthed hugely valuable material written by Richard that helps us understand parts of this family's life that was previously missing.

Ayanda Hlabisa I thank my associate Ayanda Hlabisa who competently looks after the business side of UmSinsi Press and of the Dancing Pencils Literary Development Project.

Vera Castleman who created the family tree from information given to her and who typeset this book.

Posthumously we thank **Donald McLeod** for his writing on the Byrne Valley and Constance Ivy MacLeod for her records.

We acknowledge **Dr Ruth Gordon** for her "Dear Louisa" book. This book is an important starting point for anyone interested in the history of the voyage of the *Minerva* and what happened to the families who settled in the Byrne Valley. It was published by Dr Ruth Gordon in 1970. Letters written by Ellen McLeod to her sister Louisa McLeod in England were fortunately preserved and made available to Dr Gordon. Some of them had been transcribed by members of the McLeod family. They cover the years 1850 to 1888 when Ellen McLeod died.

The letters were passed around the family in England so a few of them are missing. Unfortunately Louisa's replies were not preserved - they probably came to grief through fires and insect attack. Dr Gordon gives an idea of what was going on in the wider world outside the Byrne Valley. The dangers of pioneer life, the fevers and hostile tribes encountered by transport- riding young men, are described. along with accounts of the farming life they were all involved in, and the flowers Ellen planted with seeds sent by Louisa to create a beautiful garden.

We **thank Leonard Baumann** for memories and insights given to us.

The cover design, back and front cover are by **Thariq Kader** and myself.

Author profile

Felicity Keats Morrison

I was born on 3 February 1933 and christened as Felicity Anne Lloyd. In 1955 I married Leslie Richard Keats, from whom I separated in 1990. We had four children – Jocelyn, Lesley-Anne, Hilton and Brian. In 1996 I married Stuart Angus Morrison, known as Sam. He passed away in 2002. I have twelve grandchildren, eleven from my marriage to Les, and one step grandchild from my marriage to Sam.

I was twenty eight years old when I fell in love with writing and am still in love with it. I took many short courses to learn the craft and for a number of years I had limited success as a freelance writer. During the 1960s for almost seven years I was editor and sub editor of the South African Bee Journal. I was excited about honeybees and this led to the publication of my first children's book, *The Wild Swarm,* published by Tafelberg in 1988. The information in the book was so vital for children that Tafelberg had it translated into Afrikaans and it came out as *Die Wilde Swerm* in 1989. And in 1990 Tafelberg published another teenage novel of mine, *Rudolf's Valley*, which was set on Lily Glen in the Byrne Valley, fictionalized of course.

Changes in South Africa leading to the democracy meant changes in what publishers published. I took a break from submitting manuscripts and turned my attention to teaching writing, first just a few adults and then to teaching children. It was by doing this that I discovered the secret of accessing the creative right side of the brain. My students who previously had not had success in achieving publication in the media, were doing so; I realised they needed a platform from which to be heard so in 1995 I registered a publishing company, UmSinsi Press cc, and our first two anthologies of adult stories were published. I then turned to writing and publishing children's stories and those written by children who had right brain training. By the year 2022 UmSinsi Press had more than two thousand published books on its lists. More than half the titles were written by teens and preteens. Amongst the publications was perhaps my most important book, called *Dancing Pencils* and published in 1999 it gave out the secret of accessing the right side of the brain.

Much water has gone under my bridge with the development of a right brain adult mentor programme enabling the right brain knowledge to reach the deepest rural areas and so uplift literacy levels. In 2022 another important book of mine was published. *Gum Tree Classrooms ... the power of education,* in which I tell the story of how in one hour using WhatsApp with video I trained a principal in Uganda and ten of his school pupils who wanted a writing club, to write publishable work. We then

Zoom trained a local school to twin with the Uganda school and to write publishable work. This has resulted in a zoom master mentor programme I now run.

Amongst UmSinsi published books are more than thirty by myself, all of different genre. Children's stories, teachers' right brain writing guides, auto biographies of journeys in the physical training of writing, and now this biography.

I have also written ten adult fictional novels under the nom de plume of Catherine de Waal, with the name slightly borrowed from my Lloyd ancestry. Some of my books are available on Amazon as Kindle books.

Felicity's children circa 1968

From left Hilton, Lesley Ann, Brian and Jocelyn

Pat McLeod, Felicity and her three older children (Jocelyn, Lesley Ann and Hilton)

Felicity's Grandchildren

Granddaughters from left: Ashley McLaren, Gen Chorn, Caitlin Summers (Keats), Erin Keats and Morgan Keats

Brett McLaren

Mitchell Chorn

Calvin Keats

Dominic Keats

Charlie Keats

Step granddaughter Emily Morrison

Matthew Keats

Author profile

Mary MacLeod Hall

I was born in Surrey to parents who were second cousins descended from Scottish ancestors and I believed I was a Scot. This resulted in an interest in all things Scottish, country dancing, joining a Scottish choir, climbing Scottish mountains, eventually living near Edinburgh, then in Perthshire.

Having been evacuated to a Catholic boarding school to avoid London bombing in WW2 and having studied history at Leeds University, I became interested in the history of the Scottish Episcopal Church which I joined in the Edinburgh area. The only writing I have done is for magazines produced by two of the churches I have belonged to: co-editing a magazine for a church near Edinburgh, and later co-editing and writing articles for a magazine for a group of Episcopal churches in Perthshire. I married and after twenty three years separated from my half-Scot husband. We had two children; my daughter is an amateur musician living and playing Scottish traditional music in the area bordering Perthshire and Stirling, my son lives in Paris and has four children who enjoy visiting Scotland with its rain and midges - - and sometimes gorgeous weather.

I taught history (badly) in a school in Cheshire, later worked in the housing department of the New Town of Livingston. After retirement, with my daughter and her husband I ran a backpackers' hostel for a few years in Perthshire. I still live near there.

Voluntary work connected with the church has been good: in the 1990s there was a project giving practical help to people affected by HIV/AIDS in Edinburgh. Now I co-ordinate the activities of a group of churches in East Perthshire. Other interests have been gardening, trying to be nearly self-sufficient in fruit and vegetables, hill walking, dog-walking and looking after other people's dogs; reading, which includes a large number of books inherited from my father's family. During the years 2003 until 2019 I travelled the length and breadth of the UK in a small camper-van, initially trying to visit places where I knew family members had lived: MacLeod's in Yorkshire, Newcastle and Edinburgh, and my father's mother's side in Essex and Suffolk. I went to South Africa for three months in 1996-7 and with help from my cousins was able to visit places which my mother, who had been born there, had known.

People said I should write a book, but I knew I wouldn't have the time or patience to do the research required!

Author profile

Gwynyth Wendy Johnson

I was born in Bellair, Durban in 1944. I am married and have two children and four grandchildren, presently all living in Australia.

I went to the local Bellair Primary School followed by Durban Girls' High School. After finishing school, I trained at the IBM Education School in Johannesburg as a Computer Programmer and Systems Analyst.

I enjoyed a career working at IBM in both Johannesburg and Durban. The job included writing programs, designing systems, and documenting them. Writing sales proposals and providing education for customers.

I worked at the IBM Laboratory in Rochester, Minnesota on a two month assignment where I was a co-author of an IBM Red Book, a technical book on the first release of SQL Software on the IBM AS/400 computer, which was published in 1988.

Since retirement on the Northern Beaches of Sydney, Australia, I have been an active member of the Arthur Ransome Society and regularly contributed articles and Activity Reports to the Furthest South newsletter.

I have had an interest in Family History for many years, taking over the correspondence my mother was having with Margaret Lloyd of Grahamstown and keeping the published Lloyd Family Tree book "The Family of Henry James and Rebecca Lloyd" up to date with "Hatched, Matched and Despatched" information.

I have been contributing to Wikitree for the past eight years. I have added over two hundred ancestor profiles to the World Wide Wikitree System, and have made over two thousand five hundred contributions to existing profiles.

Author profile

Sandra (Sandi) Lynn Koenig

I was born in Durban in June 1966. I currently live in Ballito on the beautiful KZN coast. I married my husband Maurice in 1991 and we have three children. Our eldest Max (twenty five) is living in Cape Town and is completing his articles to qualify as a Chartered Accountant. Our daughter Jodie (twenty three) has just graduated as a Mechatronic Engineer at the University of Stellenbosch and our youngest, Emily (twenty one) graduated in 2022 with a Bachelor of Commerce, also from Stellenbosch University and will be doing her Honours in Financial Management in 2023. All three of our children are musical and play a variety of musical instruments, including piano, saxophone, clarinet, guitar, ukulele and harmonica. Max and Emily were both members of the Stellenbosch University Choir, which is the oldest and most celebrated choir in South Africa and is currently ranked number 1 on the Interkultur World Ranking List of the top one thousand international choirs. A talent perhaps inherited from their McLeod ancestors.

My husband Maurice recently retired from the Financial Sector. Having studied Computer Science (Information Systems), I worked in IT for many years, taking a break when my children were growing up. I currently work part time and remotely as the Company Secretary for a private nature reserve in the KZN Midlands. Maurice and I enjoy an active, outdoor life and travelling, in South Africa, Africa and abroad.

I spent my formative years in Mandini, Zululand. My brother Donald and I had a wonderful upbringing with freedom to explore our country surroundings on foot and bicycle. We had a weekend house at Drummond which is in the Hammarsdale area. My father who was a McLeod descendant, had strong ties to this area. I don't ever recall visiting his childhood home or retracing his childhood footsteps, but I'm sure we must have done so in the early days of buying the land at Drummond and building the house. Often, if my brother and I displayed any sign of being ungrateful teenagers, my father would remind us how he walked to school and back every day - at least a mile through long grass, barefoot and in all weather conditions (the proverbial *in my day* . . .). Donald and I would roll our eyes, as only teenagers can do, knowing deep down that this was not an exaggeration. My father was very emotional when it came to family matters, not having had much of a family life in his youth. He shed a tear at our graduations - particularly when Donald followed in his footsteps and qualified as an Engineer; and my husband Maurice clearly recalls his future father in law's lip quivering as he walked me down the aisle on our wedding day and lifted my veil to kiss me on the cheek.

Our cousins on our mother's side were older than us and were scattered across South Africa. On my father's side we had one cousin, Anthony (Tony) Orbin who was also much older than us and we didn't see much of him. My father was very fond of his brother Teddy, but they were not particularly close; possibly because they had lived apart from an early age - from his early teens my father moved between family members and boarding houses. Surprisingly my father and Teddy were remarkably similar - both in looks and in hobbies (they both loved and were exceptionally good at woodworking) and they did connect from time to time and compare notes.

On our weekend trips to our cottage in Drummond we would often stop by spontaneously at our Keats and Lloyd cousins in Malvern and Escombe respectively. We particularly loved visiting the Keats home at Hollings Road as they had a large swimming pool. I fondly remember "Tanglewood" the family home at 1 Hollings Road, Uncle Hector and his incredible ability to imitate bird sounds, and Auntie Vera in her wheelchair. They were my father's *family* and were very important to him. Having grown up effectively without parents, he considered Felicity, Michael and younger sister Gwyn as his siblings. In particular, Felicity. As such, they became our extended family too and we are grateful that they always welcomed us into their home with a smile and a cup of tea! Furthermore, my brother Donald was christened "Donald Richard Hector Orbin" after Uncle Donald, Uncle Hector and of course my father, Richard!

I have thoroughly enjoyed the process of delving into my McLeod ancestry. Auntie Felicity and I poured over the contents of a huge box of photos and letters. I was especially intrigued by the little black notebook that Herbert McLeod kept from 1917 to 1939, in which he recorded every little detail, such as how long a bar of Lifebuoy soap, or a box of matches lasted; and when he purchased boot laces, braces, Vaseline, singlets etc. Every purchase and each gift were meticulously recorded with the date and price. Gifts were always practical items, such as socks, handkerchiefs, braces, vests and even two coils of wire netting from Vera for Christmas in 1931. The most luxurious gift I saw in the notebook was a brass fountain pen he received from his daughter Evelyn (my grandmother) on 4th May 1927. It's a pity that all the entries were so *clinical*. Even the death of Herbert's wife, Florence, on 8th August 1937, was simply recorded as "Florence passed away".

I was also intrigued by the numerous letters written between family members, on paper so delicate it feels as if it will fall apart in your hands. The small, curvy handwriting is meticulous and quite difficult to decipher. Reading these letters, I felt as if I was prying into their lives. They have however, provided valuable insight into the past and it has been an honour for me to be part of this wonderful process.

Sandi and Donald growing up in Mandini

Sandi and her father Richard Orbin

Max, Jodie and Emily Koenig performing at various functions

Timeline for the family of Herbert McLeod and Florence Baumann

1813	Ellen Cristall born
1814	George More McLeod born
1824	JF Baumann (JFB) born Niederstetten, Wurttemberg (7/5/1824)
1842	Mary-Ann Cole born Leytonstone, England
1850	George and Ellen McLeod arrived on *Minerva*, ship-wrecked off the Bluff, moved to Byrne Valley
1851	JFB arrives in Durban
1855	Herbert born "Rose Cottage", Byrne
1861	Mary Ann Cole arrived in Durban
1864	Mary Ann Cole married JF Baumann
1868	Florence born in Leytonstone, Essex
1875 - 1879	Florence living in Hong Kong
1881	George More dies and Herbert takes over the farming
1884	Florence arrives in Durban to live with her father JF Baumann
1886	Florence goes to Byrne first to help Frank and Annie McLeod with the children and then to "Rose Cottage" as companion to Ellen McLeod

1888	Herbert marries Florence Baumann
1888	Marion Eleanor "Maisie" born in Byrne
1890	Evelyn Irene born in Byrne
1892	Ivor Herbert born in Byrne
1893	Family leaves Rose Cottage, goes to Durban and lives at "Lilybank" in Bellair where they try growing tropical fruit. Herbert works at the Railways Office in Durban
	Ivor christened in Bellair
1897	JFB dies
1897	Leave "Lilybank" and buy "Rosedene" in Ethelbert Rd, Malvern
1897	Doris Jessie born in Malvern
1897	Doris dies and is buried in Malvern Cemetery
1899	Ivor dies and is buried in Malvern Cemetery
1900	Sometime in 1900, after her husband, Mr Marsh dies, Mary Ann Cole moves to Malvern to live with Florence and Herbert
1901	Hector Percy born in Malvern
1904	Constance Ivy born in Malvern
1907	Vera Edna born in Malvern

1909	Mary Ann Cole dies and is buried in Malvern Cemetery beside the children, Doris and Ivor.
1906 – 1916	Hector, Constance and Vera attend Malvern Primary School
1913	Marion marries Thomas Lee
1914	Florence Elizabeth May Lee born
1916	Marion has a breakdown as a result of fear of Germans and her German ancestry. Tom Lee goes to war and Marion ends up in mental hospital in PMB. May lives with Florence and Herbert as a small child. May lives with Tom Lee and his second wife Edith
1917	Florence buys a shop at 435 Point Rd and Florence goes to manage it
	Vera goes to Bulwer Park Primary School
	Connie goes to Durban Girls' High School
	Hector goes to Cedara Agricultural College
1918	Herbert moves whole family from Malvern to 435 Point Road
1919	Herbert sells business at 435 Point Rd and moves family to new premises at 556 Point Rd where Florence has a shop
1918	Bessie dies on 5th August 1918. On 31/7/1918 Herbert records "heard that Bessie is very bad now not likely to survive"

1918	Evelyn working at Nels Rust Creamery
1919	Evelyn marries Ben Orbin and lives in Wyebank
1920	Florence buys a small farm in Harrison in anticipation of Herby retiring from Railways, and on 5th January 1920 Florence, Connie and Vera go to Harrison and lodge at a farm nearby. Herbert commences building a house on Harrison property which takes a year to complete
1920	Vera is taken out of school at end of Primary School education and in her words "dumped in the country" in Harrison
1920	Connie wins Acutt scholarship and goes to University in PMB. She boards at a house in PMB with Snib Cocker-Hall (Sweeney)
1920	Hector at Cedara Agricultural College
1920	Evelyn's son Teddy born in Wyebank
1921	Herbert retires from railway aged 65 and on 1/1/1921 he moves from 556 Point Rd to the Harrison house that Florence named "Leytonstone", after her birthplace and as it was "late" and built of stone
1922	20th June 1922 - Sale of Point Road property from Mrs SFA McLeod to Mr J Hunter. Selling price £1600

1923	Herbert writes in 1923 that a man came to see Harrison property but said "much too dear" at £1800 as going concern. (Author's note: perhaps he considered selling if the price had been right?)
1924	Evelyn's son Richard born at Yorkshire Nursing Home in Durban
1924	Connie teaching at Eshowe
1924	Herbert and Florence buy a farm in Hammarsdale for Hector and he proceeds to build a new house around 1928/9. Handmade all the cement blocks with the help of only one labourer. He called it Zephyr Ridge
1925	Ben Orbin writes to Evelyn that he is going to travel to the USA to try and get a disability pension from injuries sustained in WW1, and never returns. He dies in the USA on 22nd July 1926
1926ish	Vera meets Frank Lloyd at Cliffdale Tennis club
1927/8	Vera living with Evelyn at Wyebank while she is at Tech Art College – paid for by Connie
1928	Connie teaching in Eshowe
1929	Vera and Frank marry and move to Nottingham Road

1929	Connie teaching at Rossburgh and living in Durban at Quadrant House, and enjoying life
1929	Herbert and Florence still living at Harrison and visited by Connie and Hector after "slow train" ride from Durban. It seems that Teddy and Richard were living with their grandparents Herbert and Florence at Harrison before 1929. RHO said his earliest memory was living with them
1929	Evelyn still living at Wyebank - visited by Connie
1929	Teddy and Richard go to live with Hector at Zephyr Ridge. Richard hasn't started school yet
	Evelyn working in the office at Durban Station. According to Richard's memoirs the boys went by train to Cato Ridge School. Richard aged 6 and Teddy 10. They had to walk a long way barefoot to Hammarsdale station to get to school
1930	Florence writes to Vera from Leytonstone saying they have "advertised for a few children as we have Teddy and Richard – a few more would not be much more trouble"
1933	Felicity born in February while Vera and Frank living in Kloof

1933	Herbert and Florence move to live with Hector at "Zephyr Ridge" Hammarsdale. Letter from Connie hoping they will be "happier in their new home"
1933	Vic Evans suggests that Connie apply for teacher exchange programme in England. So, in 1933 Connie goes to England on this Exchange program and meets 2nd cousin, Donald MacLeod and other McLeod relatives. Donald shows her around
1934	Connie returns to SA and teaches at Inchanga. Meets and makes disastrous marriage to Clement Langton, goes to London with him and is abandoned there. Helped by cousin Donald MacLeod and remains in England
1935	Michael born in March while the Lloyd family live in Mariannhill
1935	Mary born in England to Connie and Donald MacLeod
1936	Letter from JML Baumann addressed to Mr and Mrs F McLeod "Zephyr Ridge" Hammarsdale
1937	Florence and Herbert living with Hector at "Zephyr Ridge" Hammarsdale
1937	Florence dies 8th August 1937 of Pneumonia after ambulance takes her to PMB and is

	buried at Cato Ridge. Herbert lives at Mariannhill with Vera and Frank for a few months then moves to Old Age Home
1941	Herbert dies aged 86 on 25th June 1941 in Durban and is buried with Florence at Cato Ridge
1942	Evelyn worries that Teddy might go to war. Her Wyebank house burns down, and she has a breakdown. Visits Vera in Dickens Rd, Bellair, and subsequently moves to PMB mental hospital. Ted working for Bakers in Durban and Richard is at Durban Tech High School, both living in boarding houses in Durban
1945/6	Hector leaves farming and Hammarsdale and goes to work as a chemist at Illovo Sugar Mill

Another Lifetime

Felicity Keats

Historical Map of South Africa

The old maps of South Africa are from an old Phillips School Atlas from 1957. The first map shows South Africa and the Cape Colony from 1806 when the British gained control of the Cape from the Dutch, up until 1840 when the Great Trek was underway – Dutch colonists trying to get out of reach of the British Administration. All to no avail as the second map shows the various annexations of parts of South Africa as the British controlled borders moved further and further north, until the Union of South Africa was declared in 1910.

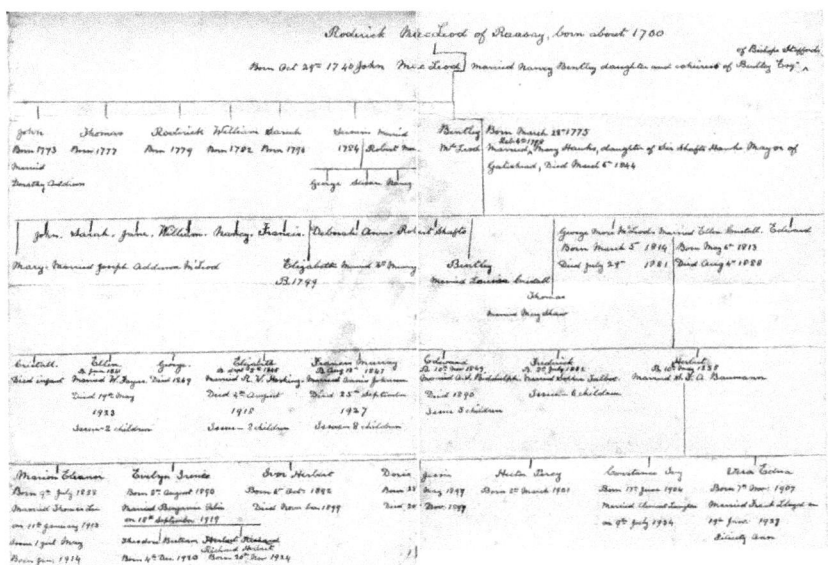

Family tree from 1700 by Herbert McLeod

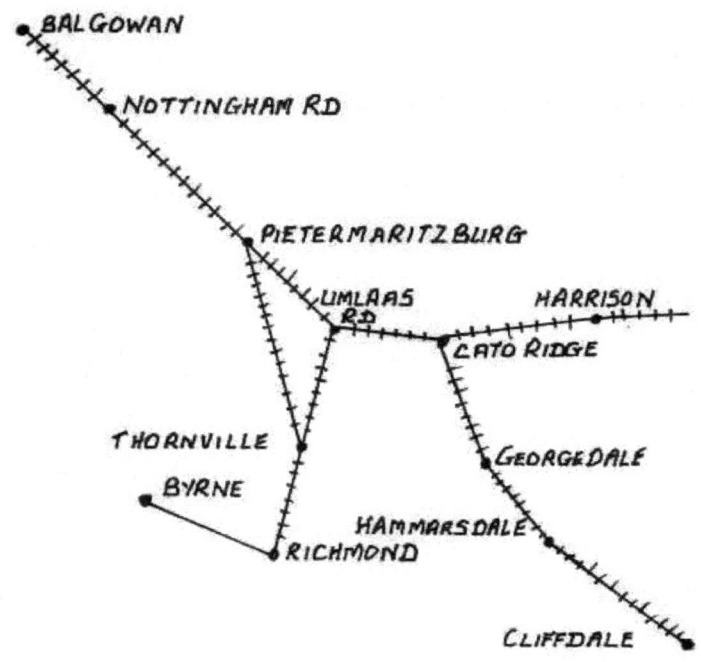

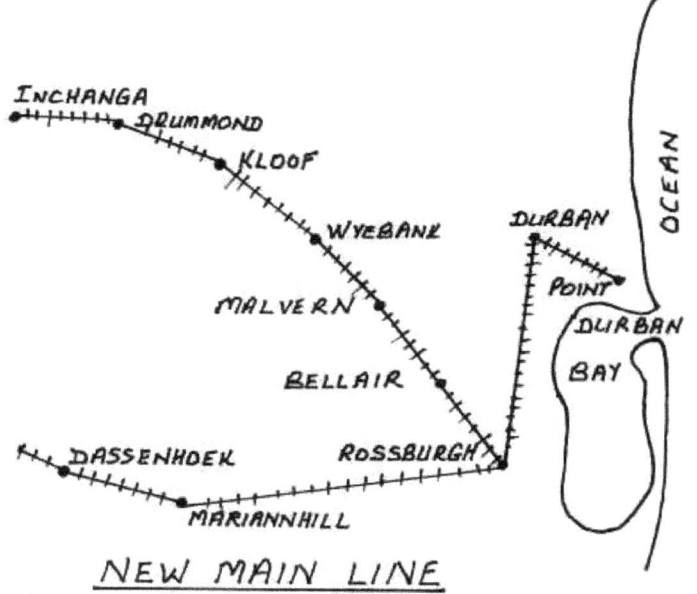

Family Tree Of People Involved In This Book

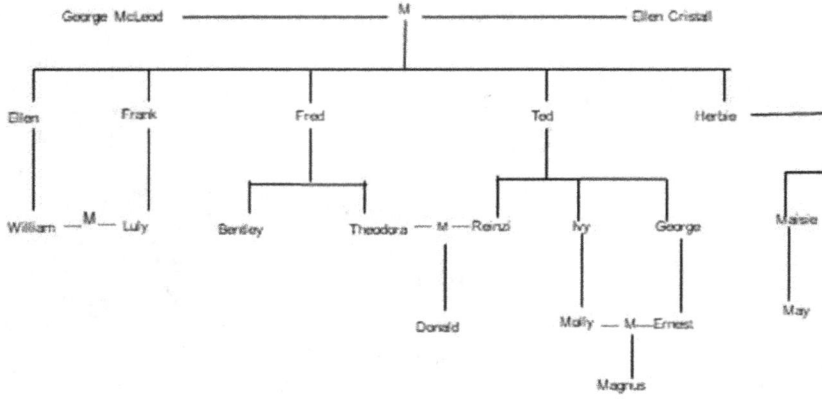

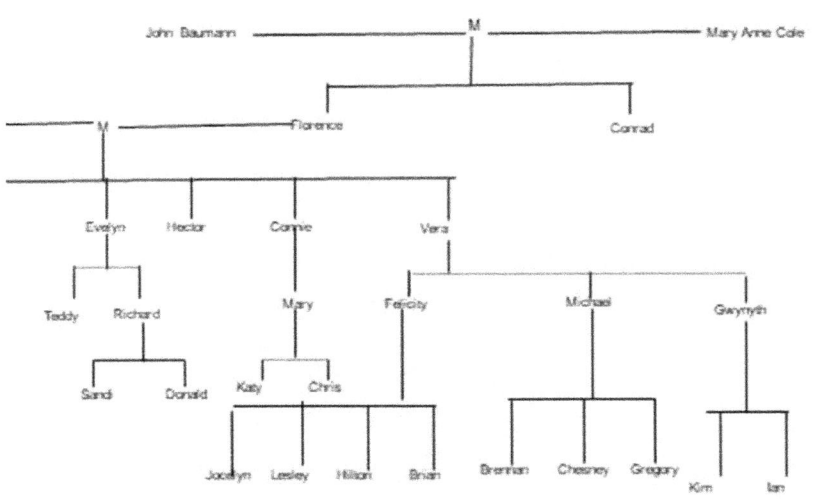

Chapter 1

Introducing Mary Ann Cole

My great grandmother on my mother's side was Mary Ann Cole. Joseph Cole her father was a jeweller in Leytonstone, England, with his home above his shop. With his wife Sarah, he had nine children with Mary Ann the oldest of them all. She was born in 1842.

Mary Ann had light blue eyes a fair complexion and light brown hair and was said to be light-hearted and friendly.

1860 Mary Ann Cole 18 years old

In 1861, when she was nineteen years old, she went with her aunt and uncle, James Lambert, to Durban South Africa as companion to her aunt. Her uncle had got a contract to harden the road, Point Road, from the harbour to the town centre.

Her uncle however had badly miscalculated the difficulties and the costs involved and he went bankrupt.

During her time in Durban she had met a German baker John Fredrick Baumann who was considerably older than she but he was captivated by her. He was interested in marrying Mary Ann and when her uncle found that he didn't have enough money left to pay her boat fare back to England, he suggested that she accept him.

Introducing John Frederick Baumann

So, on the 7th May 1864 Mary Ann married John Frederick Baumann in the house where she lived in with her aunt and uncle in Mona Road, Durban.

We are indebted to Len Baumann for a lot of this information. Len is the grandson of JML Baumann who was Florence's cousin.

John Frederick Baumann

Johan Frederick Baumann, (JFB) known as John, was born in Rohrenbrunnengasse in Niederstetten, Wurttemberg on 7th May 1824 and probably trained as a baker, although his father was a shoemaker. Baumanns still live in this house.

During the early 1800s, after the end of the Napoleonic Wars and the Dissolution of the Holy Roman Empire, the country that is present day Germany was a Confederation of many small Germanic Duchies and Principalities and four larger Kingdoms, but growing discontent with the political and social order resulted in the outbreak of revolutions in 1848.

We don't know exactly when John (JFB) left Niederstetten which was in the Kingdom of Württemberg, but it is likely that he left, aged twenty four, at the time of these revolutions. He emigrated to England and settled in Hull for three years. He became a British Citizen during this time, and changed the pronunciation of his Baumann name from "Bough-man" to "Bowman."

Times were hard in Yorkshire at that time, and Natal was looking for British Colonists. There was a lot of emigration from Leeds and Hull between 1849 and 1852 to Natal, including JFB, who seems to have been an adventurous young man. He sailed aboard *The John Bright*, from London and landed in Durban on 8th May 1851, his 27th birthday.

His name appeared on the Passenger List as:

Bowman. John F. Baker

Durban was a small town of about one thousand residents when John arrived.

He was an enterprising man and in December 1851 he started his own Bakery and Confectionery business in West Street. He moved premises several times over the next ten years, in West and Smith Streets, before being declared bankrupt in 1862. By the following year he had taken over another bakery run by E Kermode and a flour dealership.

The records show that John was active in the community and a regular advertiser in the Natal Mercury newspaper.

He joined the Philharmonic Society in 1853 as a founder member, and became a member of the Royal Durban Rangers. And in 1856 he catered for a picnic celebrating the end of the Crimean War.

In 1865 he installed a Stephens Patent Bread Machine in his bakery, which mechanised the kneading of the bread dough, saving time and labour and improving cleanliness.

And in 1864 he married Mary Ann Cole.

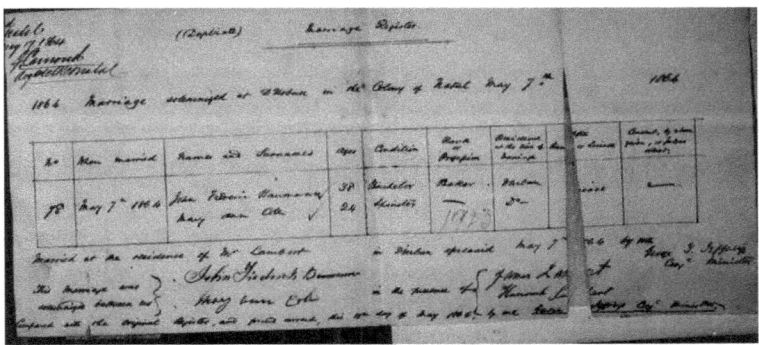

Duplicate copy of Wedding Register – JFB and Mary Ann Cole Durban 7th May 1864 at the residence of Mr Lambert

Niederstetten Baumann Family Home

1965 Baumann Family Group in Niederstetten

***

Len Baumann sent a story to Gwyn Johnson on 16th October 2022. This story was told to Len when he was about twelve by his grandfather JML Baumann. Johan Michael Leonard was known as Leonard and was Florence's cousin.

When I was a lad of about 12 years my grandfather told me that when he was a boy there was no such country as Germany, and then gave me the story.

In the north in Europe there was Prussia and down south was Austria. Somewhere in between was the Kingdom of Wurttemberg (where all my grandparents and all the Baumanns, including my mother were born in the town of Niederstetten) with its own King, Royalty and so on, similar to England.

Then in 1870 the Prussians under Bismarck invaded the Kingdom. Grandpa said at the age of sixteen he was standing in the street in Niederstetten when Bismarck rode through with his army. Grandpa took an instant dislike to the haughty man, decided he did not want to live under such a person and so next year renounced his citizenship of Württemberg. He became stateless. I have the original document

He travelled on a barge down the Rhine and ended up in London's East End where he got a job in a bakery. In time he acquired British citizenship and finally owned his own bakery. He never at any time had German Nationality. Germany was created later. He was in London for about 7 years. It was there that he had the chance meeting with his unknown Uncle John visiting England from Africa. John had left Württemberg some 40/45 years earlier and had settled in Hull in England before sailing to Africa and was presumed dead by the family. So John also never had German nationality but became a British colonist in Africa.

Quite a history!

***

Mary Ann's Pregnancies

It wasn't long before Mary Ann was pregnant and her first son Frederick was born on 1st April 1865. Not long after that she was again pregnant and her second son, Conrad Joseph was born in May 1866. But Mary Ann had a difficult birth and with just a midwife present, the birth was long and painful. The baby when he was born was injured during the birth process and remained sickly all his life.

In 1867 when Mary Ann discovered she was pregnant again she asked her husband John if she could engage the services of a doctor for the birth. He disagreed saying that the midwife was all she needed. Mary Ann then decided to return to England and to her parents' home where she would have the care and professional facilities she needed during childbirth.

She left young Fredrick with his father and took the sickly Conrad with her. Her daughter was born in Leytonstone England on 9th January 1868. Mary Ann called her Sarah Florence Amelia after some of her sisters. She and Conrad and the baby settled down to live with her parents.

However, a combination of factors inclined Mary Ann to look for employment to help maintain her two children and herself. As she had a love of the sea, she found a job as a stewardess on a steam ship that visited many different countries. She left Conrad and Florence with her parents who enjoyed their grandchildren. Florence and

Conrad had a happy time with them whilst their mother was at sea.

On the first voyage a passenger who had given birth to a baby found she could not feed it. Mary Ann who had just given birth herself offered to feed the baby and the baby survived.

There were lots of stories which Florence, at a much later stage of her life, told her daughter Connie about Florence's life in England. Florence had the dark brown eyes of her German father and a browner complexion than the fair English aunts, so her grandfather named her "Toppie" from the popular story of Topsy the little black girl. At supper time he would say "Toppie, Toppie, Toppie, mind the fish bones" in case she choked on the bloaters they often ate.

In the home was a small Pomeranian dog called Fan that was constantly tricked by a parrot. The parrot would imitate the grandmother's voice and call "Fan Fan Fan" and the dog would pelt downstairs. The parrot would then laugh, ha ha ha, and Fan would realise that he had again been caught out and would sheepishly go back upstairs.

***

John and Fredrick – off to the Goldfields

Meanwhile back in South Africa in 1874, Mary Ann's husband John Baumann had taken their son Fredrick and gone to the gold fields in the Transvaal. On the way there they developed a dreadful fever and the transport driver had left them at a roadside hostelry, sure they would both die.

Mary Ann's ship called in at various countries and ports such as countries like Australia and cities like San Francisco, Hong Kong and Durban. And when she was in Durban in about 1875 Mary Ann had tried to contact her husband John Baumann. However she had also heard the story that they were probably both dead so considered herself a widow. What was more, a monthly allowance that she had been getting from her husband had stopped and this too had her believing he was probably dead.

John and Fredrick however had survived and had made their way to Pilgrim's Creek where John had set up a catering business with John Stopforth to supply meals to the miners. He had left his Durban business in the hands of a manager, asking him to send regular amounts of money on a monthly basis to Mary Ann but the manager had embezzled it.

***

Anecdote about JF Baumann in Pilgrims Rest, Eastern Transvaal Goldfields. 1874.

In his book "Reminiscences of a South African Pioneer", WC Scully records the following which appears to refer to about 1874.

"Before very long a few diggers came and prospected in the vicinity of the saddle for surface gold. Among them was one of the strangest characters I have ever met. His name was John

Mulcahy. Mulcahy and I first met at the Rotunda Creek rush, and when that abode of "wild cat" collapsed, we arranged to take a prospecting trip towards the Olifant River.

We arrived at the lower camp one morning at about 9 o'clock, more than half starved. I shall never forget my wolfish sensations as we flung down our swags at Stopforth and Bowman's eating house and called for breakfast. I then enjoyed the heartiest meal of my life, after which I sat back pulling at my pipe and noting with astonishment the amount of food which Mulcahy consumed.

I thought he would never stop; plateful followed plateful in an apparently endless endeavour to sate the insatiable. However all things must come to an end; so, eventually did Mulcahy's gargantuan meal. As he paid the prescribed fee of two shillings I thought Stopforth looked pensive.

After resting for some 10 days and the weather having in the meantime cleared, we made another start. We had decided to commence our journey after a good meal so struck our tent early one morning at the Upper Creek and tramped down to the Lower Camp, once more to bestow the doubtful favour of our custom upon Stopforth and Bowman

We put down our swags at the door and entered. It was barely 8 o'clock so no other customers had arrived. The eating house was a large marquee tent, with rough tables and benches on either side of a passage down the middle. At the end of this passage a square piece had been cut out of the canvas and it was through the resulting aperture that plates were passed to and from the kitchen. Bowman it was who presided over the cooking while Stopforth did the waiting.

We took our seats at one of the tables and called for breakfast. Stopforth stood for a few seconds and regarded Mulcahy with a sombre eye. Then he strolled slowly down the passage and called through the aperture

"Bill."

"Hello"

"Breakfast for 10. Here's this son of a ...... back "

My partner was enormously pleased at this compliment to his prowess; for months afterwards he used to chuckle at the remembrance of it."

Thanks to Len Baumann for this anecdote printed in his compilation: "John Frederick Baumann. An Early Colonist of Natal. 1824-1897"

***

Mary Ann stranded in Singapore

Mary Ann who had been stranded in Durban when her uncle went broke had another experience that left her stranded when her ship called in at Singapore. She had friends there and went to have afternoon tea with them. She told them she could not stay long as the ship was due to sail at 4 pm. They however assured her there was plenty of time. It turned out they had put the clock back because to Mary Ann's horror she saw her ship sailing out of the harbour.

"We are sure a storm is brewing and it will sink tonight," her friends told her. And sure enough, it did sink with all hands on board lost.... Mary Ann herself was safe and well but in a strange land.

Mary Ann in Hong Kong

Somehow she made her way to Hong Kong where she met a very nice man she only spoke of as the Gov'nor. After a few months she married him. He kindly asked Mary Ann to return to England and bring Florence to join them, so Florence's time with Conrad and her grandparents came to an end.

En route to China Florence nearly died as their ship sailed through the Suez Canal and whilst at Port Said she got separated from her mother. It was hours in the hot sun before she found her mother and the child was prostrated with sun stroke which seemed to have kept her delicate for the rest of her life.

Family heirlooms from Hong Kong

In Hong Kong, Florence soon made friends. She went to a school run by a Mrs Grimble and had a special friend called Alice Shuster. She also had a little boyfriend Hector Samson.

There are many stories that Florence as an adult told her children about her time in Hong Kong; one being that one day when Florence was walking with her *ayah* she saw several men carrying a Palanquin which is a sedan chair supported on long poles. The palanquin was curtained. Florence was curious to see who was inside, ran across and tried to pull open the curtains. Her ayah shrieked, "No, poxy man, poxy man", and ran across and pulled her away. Apparently the person inside had smallpox which was very contagious.

Another story that Connie related to Mary was that a neighbour in Hong Kong was so horrified by the thick English clothes the child was wearing that she gave Florence's mother a length of silk to make cooler clothes.

Florence in Hong Kong aged 8 circa 1876

***

After John and Fredrick were back in Durban in 1877 they took a boat trip to London probably to look for Mary Ann who was still in Hong Kong at the time. Frederick was now thirteen years old. John who had been out of touch with everyone, in London, met by chance his nephew Johan Michael Leonard Baumann (JML), who also wasn't aware that his uncle was still alive. Florence and her mother were still in Hong Kong. The meeting with his nephew, also a baker, seems to have stimulated John to return to Durban and to take up the bakery again.

For Florence and Mary Ann, the happy Hong Kong days ended abruptly. Chinese rioters started burning houses in the European Concessions. Mary Ann and Florence were driven away to a safe part of Hong Kong, however their house was blown up by authorities to create a firebreak and prevent the spread of fires. Sadly for Mary Ann and Florence this meant they had to return to England in early 1879. Mary Ann had vowed to return to her husband in Hong Kong, however, once back in England, they learned of his death.

Mary Ann back in England

Mary Ann, Florence and Con soon moved from her parent's home into a house in Forest Gate, Essex. On his thirteenth birthday in 1879, the frail Con died.

Back in England, this time to live in great poverty in London, Florence worked in a shop, learned to sew heavy bedlinen, earning very little money. One night in 1879 crouching over a tiny fire, after her mother had gone to answer the door, she received a great shock. Her mother came in with a heavy-set man and burst out, Florence this is your cousin Leonard. Your father is not dead and he wants you to go out to him in Durban. Florence still a child (around eleven years old) did not want to leave her mother so refused.

Mary-Ann Cole undated

Again in 1879, John Baumann suggested that Leonard, as his nephew was always called, should join him in partnership. Just married to Marie Kurz, Leonard decided to do so, and went out to Durban. Money was put into the business, more Baumann relatives came in, and the business grew. But sadly the original founder, John, found himself gradually more and more indebted to Leonard and "taken over". Lonely and ill, he began to wish for his daughter. Leonard undertook to go to London to find her.

Introducing Florence

At first Florence was not inclined to agree, but at last she did and in November 1884 she landed in Durban. The experiment was a disaster! Florence had been out in the world, selling haberdashery in a shop and now her father wanted her to go back to school, to study music in Germany. This Florence was not willing to do. She found her father very difficult to live with, the only thing they had in common was a love of music. It is said that she played the piano for him to sing. Worst of all, her father and brother were forever criticising her mother for having left them. She also disliked her cousin Leonard for taking over the business. Yet in fairness it must be said that it was his money and initiative that had built up its success.

Singing was not enough to bond them, and Florence left John's home and found a way to earn an income by giving piano lessons and sewing mattress covers for customers. Then a chance advert that she saw for a governess in the Byrne Valley to Mrs Frank McLeod, then as a companion to the elderly Ellen McLeod, changed the course of her life.

She packed her things and travelled to Byrne.

Chapter 2

Florence In Byrne

Introducing Ellen and George More McLeod

By the time that Florence arrived in Byrne, it was the stronghold of a number of McLeod families descended from Ellen and George who had arrived in Byrne in 1850.

Before we look at Florence Baumann's life in Byrne, let's explore the lineage of George More McLeod and his wife formerly Ellen Cristall. Ellen had a sister in England with whom she was very close and who played a supportive role in Ellen's life in South Africa. She was Louisa.

Ellen and George More McLeod had arrived in 1850 on the sailing ship the *Minerva* that was wrecked off Durban harbour. Ellen Cristall the mother of five small children was the daughter of Joseph Cristall and Elizabeth Fox, Joseph's parents were Alexander Cristall and Anne Batten.

George More and Ellen McLeod

'Our' MacLeod History Written By Mary MacLeod (Florence's Granddaughter)

I am the daughter of Donald MacLeod from England and Constance Ivy McLeod of South Africa.

They were descended from the two older sons of the John MacLeod b 1746, John and Bentley. Donald's father was Llewellyn Wynn McLeod whose father, a son of the older one John, married Nancy Bentley McLeod the daughter of the younger one Bentley. Constance was the daughter of Herbert McLeod, whose father George More McLeod (a son of the first Bentley) took his family out to South Africa in 1850. Nancy was George More McLeod's sister.

Confused? The McLeods / MacLeods were in the habit of marrying cousins. And using the same name over and over again.

(No need to worry about the spelling of MacLeod. It matters to some people but isn't important).

Another layer to confuse us is that one of George More McLeod's brothers was Bentley McLeod who married Louisa Cristall, to whom George's wife Ellen, Louisa's sister, wrote long letters twice a year between 1850 and 1888. Two brothers married two sisters, my mother would say. These letters form the basis of the book 'Dear Louisa' by Ruth Gordon which gives us so much information about the early life of the family in South Africa.

The name Bentley occurs frequently in the family tree: this originated with the wife of the first John (b 1746)

Nancy/Ann Bentley (her Christian name was recorded differently at different times). The Bentleys came from Northowram near Halifax in Yorkshire but had moved to London where they had the brewery to which we believe John b. 1746 was sent to learn the trade, and there met Nancy/Ann Bentley whom he married.

Connection With Scotland

Clan MacLeod is a Scottish clan from Skye, Raasay, Lewis, Harris and Dunvegan and other places in the highlands and islands.

In earlier times there was much fighting between the clans, with invaders coming from the west, all seeking dominance over rival groups. But the Vikings from whom the MacLeods were descended were from the Viking Leod from Norway in the north. So we are the sons of Leod. The Vikings were superb sailors and navigated all over the known world, even reaching the land of America. Originally they came to pillage and plunder, terrorising the local inhabitants, looking for valuables, slaves and gold. Later they settled down and became farmers: good farm land was scarce in Norway. Our MacLeods claim to be descended from those who settled in Raasay.

The greatest disturbances in the 18th Century when our earliest known ancestor was born were the Jacobite Rebellions of 1715, 1719, 1722 and the worst of all 1745, culminating in the Battle of Culloden. These were attempts to restore the royal house of Stuart which had been exiled since 1688. They ended in cruel punishment for any clans or families which supported the Stuart cause. The MacLeods of Raasay had taken the Jacobite side and suffered accordingly from the London-based government. As suggested later, we do not know why or when exactly our branch of the clan moved to England and flourished as brewers in Newcastle and Gateshead in the North-east of England, some living in Edinburgh later, but none in the highlands or islands where they originated. Had they taken part in the rebellion of 1745/6? We do not know. Some remained in Scotland and the north of England, but the branches with which we are concerned, the descendants of John and Bentley McLeod, moved south and ended up in the south and in London. Apart from those who continued in the brewing business, they tended to go into the law. Llewellyn Wynn McLeod was a solicitor, so was my father. Others became barristers, as did another son and grandson of the older Bentley McLeod, Joseph Addison McLeod I and Joseph Addison McLeod II.

St Mary's Church where the Gateshead families worshipped. There is a Hawks family plot in the graveyard. The church is now a museum/heritage site.

Picture of Worsall Hall - birthplace of George More McLeod. Picture taken by Mary Hall in 2011

Worsall is near Yarm in North Yorkshire. When Magnus and Byrne McLeod were asked what they were doing in north Yorkshire : the answer was 'Being gentlemen!'

This was Bentley and Mary Hawks's family. John and Dorothy Eleanor Addison lived in Kirklevington Grange not far away.

Bentley McLeod and his wife Mary Hawks

The name Addison came from Eleanor Dorothy Addison who married the John b 1773, eldest son of the original John b 1746.

I was proud of the fact that when we, my husband Tom and I and daughter Catherine, soon joined by our baby son Christopher, moved to the Edinburgh area in 1970, I was the first one to come back to Scotland! (Another one came later, Catriona Christie who lives in Perthshire. She is a great granddaughter of Llewellyn Wynn McLeod).

Catherine, now Katy, lives near Killin which is highland. Christopher lives in Paris, but one of his daughters, Josephine aged seventeen, says she wants to live in Scotland!

Before that when we lived in the Manchester area, we were heavily into Scottish country dancing circles - all our friends were exiled Scots or children of exiled Scots. Tom had a Scottish dance band, and Katy has followed on, playing the accordion and bass.

Reading my own records of family history, I'm intrigued to see that Herbie, Connie's father, played the accordion, as did Teddy Orbin.

Mary's daughter, Katy and Teddy Orbin (circa 1940) playing the accordion

***

We Don't Know Where We Came From!

For Scots everywhere, the place you came from is important. But our family does not know! There is a tradition that we came from Raasay but we have no idea if this is true. There are numerous family trees done by various people, but they all get stuck at the same point in the early 18th Century; nobody knows where we came from. There are MacLeods in many places in the Highlands and Islands of Scotland and all over the world, but we do not know what families we are related to.

In 18th Century Scotland it was a matter of life and death which side you were on during and after the Jacobite rebellions. If you were on the 'wrong' side after the Stuart princes were defeated and exiled after the rebellions in 1715 and 1745 it was safer to disappear. (The MacLeods of Raasay were on the wrong side, they supported the Stuart cause) We are trying to uncover what the parents of our ancestor John MacLeod, the one we believe was baptised on 1/10/1746 in Newcastle, or the one, probably the same one, born on 29/10/ 1746, took great care to conceal where they came from. John's parents didn't tell their children. They left Scotland, and lived in Newcastle and Gateshead in the north of England. (Some returned later when it was safe to do so, and lived in Edinburgh. Later they drifted to London.) Our families in South Africa, Australia, New Zealand and England are all descended from two sons of the above John, John and Bentley MacLeod.

John McLeod 1746

Easier to travel by sea than on land, and Newcastle on the east coast would have been relatively easy to reach and settle down in, which they did, and did well - brewing!

An extract from an account supposedly by George More McLeod in 1894 runs: (John's father) saw that the Jacobite game was up and that legitimate work on behalf of the

Jacobite cause was deteriorating to smuggling and nothing much else, having a personal friend in England he decided to send his son out of harm's way and to give him a better chance than his brothers and uncles had.

> The NEW BREWERY, in Gateshead.
> JOHN M'LEOD and Co. beg Leave to acquaint their Friends and the Public, that they have erected a Brew-house near the Head of Pattle-bank, where they brew Strong Beer, Ale, and Table Beer, upon the best Plan ever practised in the North of England. Gentlemen, who may be so kind as to favour them with their Orders, may depend upon having their Families regularly furnished with each, or with any Kind, equally fine, and on the same Terms as in London.
> John M'Leod flatters himself, that his Character as a Brewer, established so many Years in Pipewelgate Brewery, will recommend the New Brewery in Gateshead to the Attention and Encouragement of all Gentlemen, Inn-keepers, Ale-house-keepers, and private Families, who wish to be supplied with the best Goods, upon the most easy Terms.
> ☞ Gentlemen may be furnished with Beer in Casks, the same in Quality with Pipewelgate Bottled Beer, at the most reasonable Price.
> February 14, 1778.

Newcastle Chronicle 21 February 1778

***

Some Background History

Jacobite Rebellions

From 1689 until 1746 there were rebellions starting with a battle in support of the exiled Stuart King James II of England. He had antagonised many people, partly because he was a Catholic, resulting in his abandoning the country and going to France in 1688. The throne was taken by the Protestant King William and his Stuart wife Mary. Those who remained loyal to James were known as Jacobites. After 1714 the Hanoverian kings succeeded to the throne, and several rebellions took place culminating in the final defeat of the Jacobites at Culloden in 1746. The consequences for the Jacobites were terrible. Cruel retribution was made by the British government. The Act of Union in 1707 had made Scotland part of Britain, not a separate country, so being a Jacobite was treason and could result in losing everything or death.

This continued until 1788 when James's grandson 'Bonnie Prince Charlie' (no longer bonnie and glamorous) died and there were no more Jacobite claimants.

I believe our ancestor might have had Jacobite sympathies, or even have been involved, and left Scotland with his family, leaving no record so nobody could find them or punish his relatives.

Otherwise, why not tell his children about their earlier life? *Mary MacLeod Hall*

***

One hundred years later, in 1850, the young family of George More McLeod left London, England, en route for Durban, South Africa, aboard the sailing ship the *Minerva*. They had been enticed into buying into the new project by Joseph Byrne of settling families in a new village of Byrne in the KZN Midlands. The McLeods were excited at the idea of their own town land for a town house and farmlands. They expected to make good and to return in time to England where Ellen had a close relationship with her sister Louisa. George More McLeod's wife was Ellen, previously Ellen Cristall.

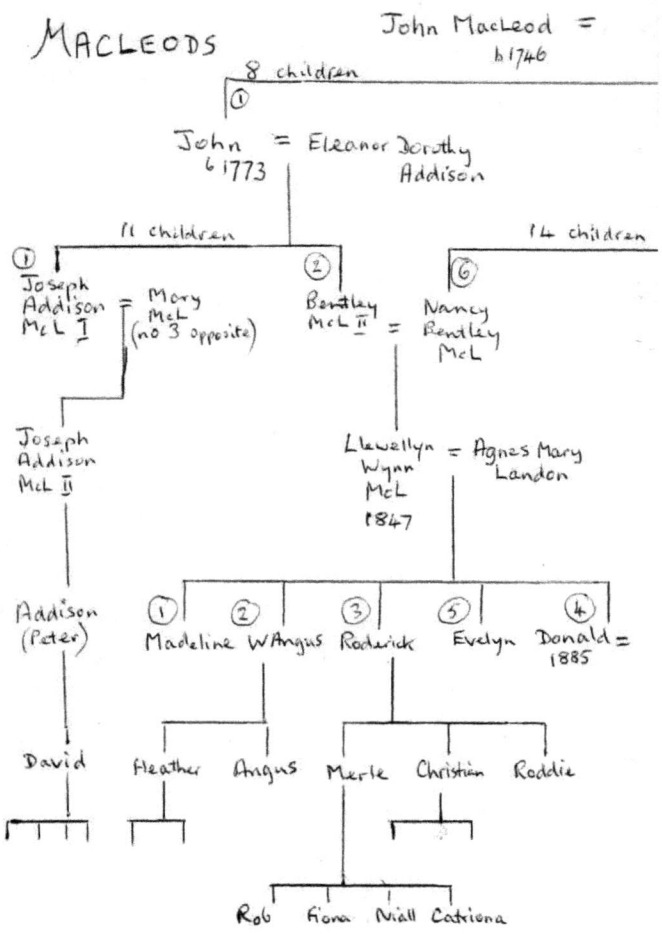

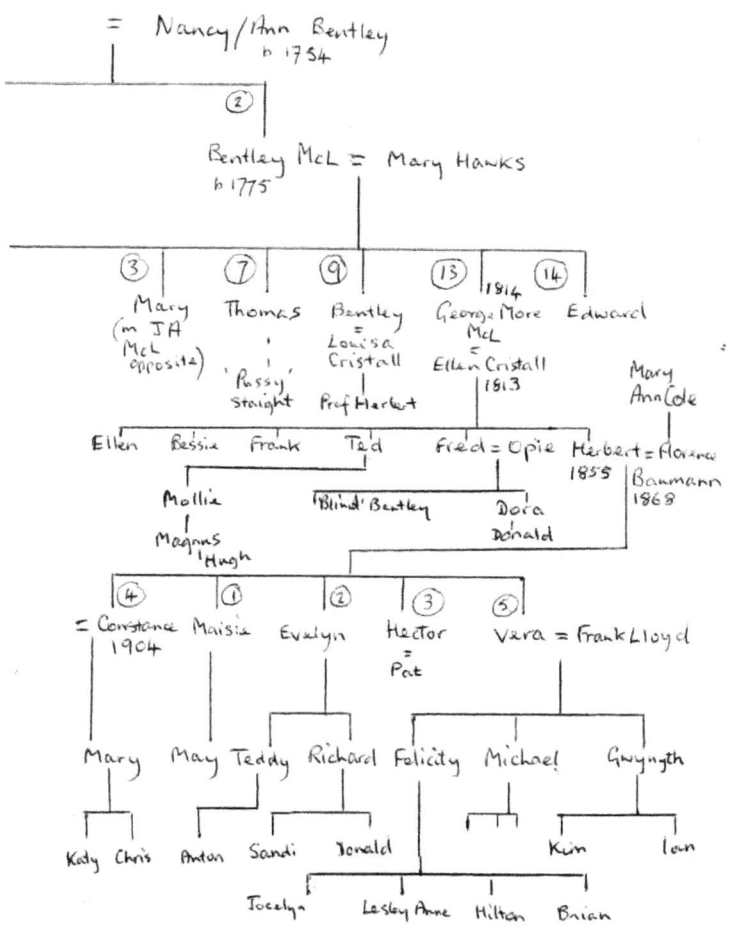

Cristall Family

Alexander Cristall (possibly Joseph Alexander Cristall) was born in about 1727 in Arbroath, Forfarshire in Scotland, which is near Perth (more Scottish Ancestry for us). He was the captain and owner of a trading vessel, and settled in Penzance, Cornwall, England, where he met and married Anne Elizabeth Batten, (born 1745) in Madron, Cornwall, on 29th April 1767.

Alexander Cristall was also a Sailmaker, and Ship Breaker, having Boatyards in Penzance and Fowey in Cornwall, and ultimately in Rotherhithe, London.

Alexander and Anne had 5 children:

Joshua	1768-1847
Ann Batten	1769-1848
Elizabeth	1771-1853
Joseph	1775-1850
Alexander	1776-1848

According to the "Dictionary of National Biography", Anne Batten is recorded as being a woman of talent and education, and had a very artistic family.

Dictionary of National Biography

CRISTALL, JOSHUA (1767–1847), painter, both in oil and water colours, was born at Camborne, Cornwall, in 1767. His father, Joseph Alexander Cristall, an Arbroath man, is believed to have been the captain and owner of a trading vessel, and also a ship-breaker, having yards at Rotherhithe, Penzance, and Fowey. His mother, Ann Batten, born in 1745, was daughter of a Mr. John Batten of Penzance, and a woman of talent and education. His eldest sister, Ann Batten Cristall, was the authoress of a volume of 'Poetical Sketches,' published in 1795. Elizabeth, a younger sister, engraved; and both sisters were most of their lives engaged in tuition. Dr. Monro was one of his early friends. He was always very fond of art and of classical music. He began life with a china dealer at Rotherhithe, and then became a china-painter in the potteries district under Turner of Burslem, living in great hardship. He became a student at the Royal Academy, and was in 1805 a foundation member of the Water-colour Society, of which body, on its reconstitution in 1821, he was also the first president; an office which he continued to hold until 1832, when Copley Fielding became his successor. His portrait in oils, a vigorous sketch painted by himself, adorns the staircase of the society's gallery.

Their son Joshua was an eminent artist in both water colours and oils and a foundation member of the Water Colour Society. Daughter Ann was the authoress of a volume of "Poetical Sketches" And their younger daughter Elizabeth was an Engraver.

Their son Joseph joined his father in the Sailmaking and Shipbreaking business and they moved to Rotherhithe on the Thames in London.

Joseph Cristall married Elizabeth Fox (born 1769) at St Dionis Backchurch, Whitechapel, London on 8th November 1796. They lived in Rotherhithe in London, England and they had eleven children, including Louisa and our great grandmother, Ellen. Ellen had a twin sister Emily who died as a baby.

Louisa probably inherited her artistic talent from her grandmother, Anne Batten.

Louisa and Ellen, married McLeod brothers Bentley and George More.

In 1841, the England Census recorded that Elizabeth and Joseph Cristall were living in Stoke Newington, Middlesex, where the McLeod family had also lived, and presumably that's where they met

***

The Wreck of the Minerva

Ellen had given birth to five children ranging in age from eight years to baby Ted who was still in arms and not yet able to walk. The children were Ellen or Dollie, aged eight, Georgie aged seven, Bessie aged six, Frank aged three and baby Ted aged ten months. But on the day they were supposed to land, with the ship anchored outside Durban harbour, a huge storm blew up. The ship broke her chain and was bashed against the rocks close to the Bluff in

Durban and eventually sank. What a horrendous night it had been! In the dark and with huge winds and heavy seas bashing the sailing vessel there had been people shouting and much chaos. Only when the dawn broke were the distraught passengers able to see the dreadful plight they were in.

Fortunately, there were more than the usual number of lifeboats on the *Minerva* and at dawn on the 4th July 1850, the work began of getting the immigrants into the lifeboats and then onto the thorn covered land below the Bluff. No lives were lost. A horse swam to shore. The settlers between them had valuable equipment like milling equipment and even collapsible houses. Though there was an attempt to save the *Minerva* by tying her masts to trees on the land, the seas and wind were too strong. On the 5th of July the *Minerva* broke up, with bits of the ship being washed up on to the shore.

The settlers were told not to take any of their possessions they might see on the shore, like cutlery, because the insurance would pay out. But the insurance didn't pay out anyway and the settlers were without money or possessions. All they had were the clothes they were wearing when they were rescued. The two oldest McLeod children Dolly and Georgie had their christening mugs in their hands when rescued. These later went onto the altar of the little wooden church the settlers built in Byrne.

The story of the McLeods as pioneer settlers in the Byrne valley is beautifully told in the book "Dear Louisa" written by Dr Ruth Gordon.

Writing was a talent and a love that many of the McLeods have. Although the settlers had lost all their possessions, at the time of the wreck Ellen had a bottle of ink in her pinafore pocket and this started a thirty eight year communication she had with her sister Louisa in England. The insurance did not pay out and the McLeods were without any possessions at all other than the christening mugs which the oldest two children had in their hands when they arrived on the shore. They slept the night on the beach and thought two children were lost only to discover them the morning, asleep under a thorn tree.

For a while they lived in a tent provided by supporters of the wreck but came the time to go to their new home in Byrne. Ellen walked the whole way, not fancying the ox cart and she carried baby Ted with her.

In Byrne they were horribly disappointed. The beautifully laid out village they had been shown in England didn't exist. Instead, there was just virgin bush. However, when one has lost everything but still has health and one's family the McLeods made the best of a bad situation. They stayed in the Byrne Valley. Other pioneer families stayed as well, and to start with they lived in an African style mud hut and used just one spoon, all taking turns to eat with it. They started to barter with the Africans for chickens. They gardened and grew vegetables. The soil in the Byrne Valley and the mists and rain were great for agriculture. George More McLeod started taking readings of rainfall and sent them in to Pietermaritzburg where they appeared in the local newspaper and became the start of the meteorological department.

Ellen and George had five children when they first arrived, Ellen later gave birth to two sons, Fred and Herbert.

Postage and paper were expensive but Ellen kept up a thirty eight year correspondence with her sister Louisa in England. Louisa was a great support for Ellen. Ellen began to list urgent items they needed. Utensils, clothing for the children and seeds to plant to grow vegetables. It took time for the letter to get by sailing ship to England and for the large box of important items to get back to Ellen and family in Byrne. The excitement at opening the box and finding shoes for the children, clothing and pots and plates must have been unbelievable.

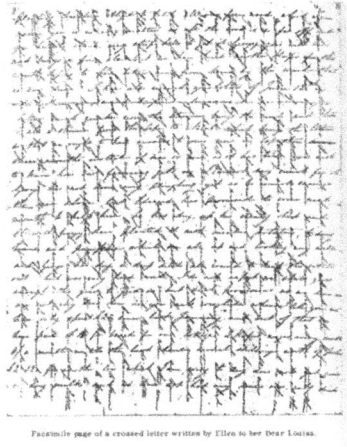

Copy of "crossed letter" scanned from the book "Dear Louisa"

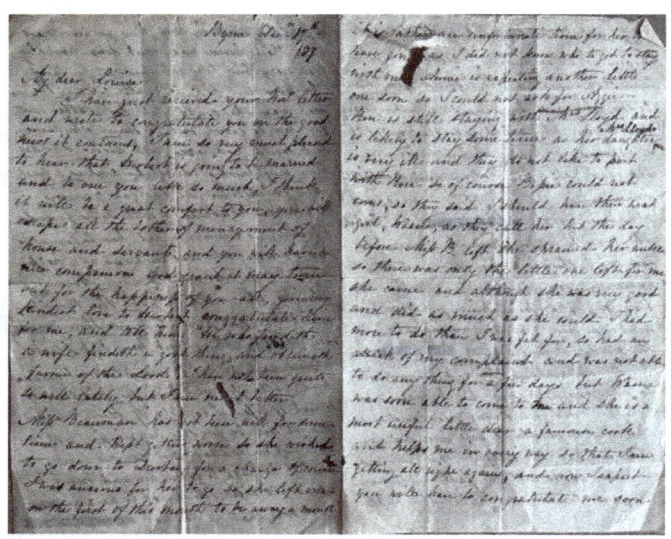

Letter from Ellen to Louisa - Byrne 19th Dec 1887
This letter was found in the family collection of letters and is not included in "Dear Louisa"

Ellen and George were both God fearing people. They knew the importance in their lives of both religion and education. They set about getting the men of the new little village to assist with the construction of a small church on ground not far from George's farmland. And they also built a small school room. The men sawed the trunks of trees into planks. One can see the saw marks in some of the floorboards still on display in for instance the Richmond Museum that has a section devoted to the influence and value of the Byrne settlers. On display are the enormous saws that two men used, one at each end, to saw these trees into planks. The first little church honoured the christening mugs of the two McLeod children which were placed in the church. Today there is a new small brick church and there is a plaque marking where the original small church stood. Also in the church grounds is a cemetery. Virtually a family cemetery as one can walk around and read the names on the headstones, and find how related these people were, one to the other.

A few tragedies did occur. Eight year old Winchester Hosking was caught in a water mill and died. His gravestone is there, in the church cemetery, as are those of most of the original settlers.

George was able to begin investing in animals. Sheep, cows and fowls so the family was able to eat fairly well though cooking on an outdoor fire was slow. George built a turf room for cooking, though Ellen battled with just one kettle and two pots to do all the cooking. To start with all they drank was water. The Africans did on occasion bring around milk for them to buy, but it was expensive. As time went on things improved.

Ellen loved gardening and grew roses at the house that George eventually built for the family on his farmland. This house he called Rose Cottage and from there went the letters in crossed writing that Ellen used to write to Louisa. The sisters were very close, and Louisa drew a beautiful pencil sketch of "The Duke of Abercorn's Children" which in about 1838 she copied from a Landseer picture and sent it to Ellen as a wedding gift. As a family we had this picture in a large mottled light brown frame hanging in our lounge for years. Then my mother decided to give it to the Macrorie House Museum where many more people would have the chance to enjoy the intricate pencil drawing.

The Macrorie House Museum ceased to exist but today there is a special corner in the Richmond Museum where this picture, now reframed has a place of honour.

And although Louisa wrote to Ellen of the elegant court functions that she attended, Ellen did not have the slightest feelings of loss or jealousy. In reply she wrote about her roses, giving them their names like *Sir this* and *Lady that*, who greeted her daily. Attention given to both religion and to education paid off. Many of those initial settlers have contributed greatly to the development of Natal. And later when Bessie, one of the children who arrived on the *Minerva* that was shipwrecked, married Richard Hosking, they built their home not far from Rose Cottage and the church, and they called it The Oaks because of the enormous oak trees that are in the front yard. Today it is a prestigious guest house that provides excellent lunches and accommodation.

Rose Cottage undated

*McLeod family picture
Evelyn, Herbert, Maisie, Tom Lee, Florence, Hector
Front: Vera, May and Connie*

1914 McLeod family - Evelyn, Herbert, Vera, Florence with baby May on her lap, and Connie

June 1925

Picnic party at Fraserdale Falls, Hammarsdale

1930 at Harrison
Vic Evans, Connie, Herbert, Vera, Frank Lloyd
Florence, Richard, Teddy and Evelyn

The McLeod children grew up and many married and built homes close to their parents. One of these was blind Bentley, son of Fred, who married Nellie. As a young teen I visited them in their home known as Blarney. Nellie had wild dark eyes and long flowing dark hair. As a teenager I noticed the dark tea stains inside the cups which obviously Bentley could not see! Bentley looked at people but his eyes were unseeing. Perhaps he had very small vision as he did amazing things, like pull tourists cars out of the mud in the road outside Blarney using a span of oxen. He also built a water mill on the river which he used to grind mealies so they had their own mealie meal.

There was another small building on the property which was Bentley's cottage. I have stayed there. On one occasion we got permission for a group of us including my cousin Mary to spend a weekend in the cottage. Mary wanted to experience what our great grandmother had experienced. She walked with Sam and Ian Morrison from Blarney to Rose Cottage along a narrow, badly rutted farm road. The write-up of our weekend in Bentley's cottage with the walk to Rose Cottage and the Oaks is in Section 2. Certainly the stories we heard about different members of the McLeod family were most inspiring.

Donald himself donated Blarney Cottage to the government as a museum for visitors to see how the settlers lived. All the bricks were handmade and there is a date on one of them showing when the house was built. Those floors show the saw marks as the wood is the original timber hand sawn by settler folk.

Donald was the son of Theodora and Rienzi who were cousins. Theodora was the daughter of Fred McLeod, and the sister of Bentley, and Rienzi was a son of Ted McLeod. Donald has also written a small book on his memories of life in Byrne which we include in our second section of this book.

Today the Byrne Valley is well laid out with streets and lovely houses. Some offer bed and breakfast accommodation and morning teas. A small stream runs through it. This is what the original settlers imagined they would be heading towards, never imagining all they would see was virgin bush.

Ellen made her mark on the history of the province in the letters she wrote to Louisa. These are in the Killie Campbell Museum in Durban and someone very carefully transcribed them so that the contents could be easily read.

Ellen was a kind and caring person, ready to help people and this is easy to see if one reads the "Dear Louisa" book.

Ellen needed help as she got older, so Florence left her job as governess for the children of Frank and Annie and moved to Rose Cottage where she took beautiful care of Ellen. It wasn't long before Florence and Ellen's son Herbert felt an attraction for one another. Florence fell pregnant and she and Herbert married in 1888, shortly before Ellen died. To start with Florence and Herbert lived in Rose Cottage. Here Florence gave birth to three children: Marion Eleanor "Maisie", Evelyn Irene and Ivor Herbert.

St Cyprians Church Wedding Register
Herbert McLeod and Florence Baumann
Durban 26th January 1888

26th January 1888
Florence and Herbert
Wedding

Florence and Herbert move from Byrne Valley

Florence admitted to Herbert she was not happy in the farming community of the Byrne Valley. She told her daughter Constance that she wasn't accepted by some members of the McLeod family. In 1893 Herbert sold Rose Cottage and the farm and they moved to Bellair in the Durban area, where for a while they unsuccessfully tried fruit farming on a property they called "Lilybank". In 1897 the family left "Lilybank" and moved to Ethelbert Road in Malvern in a house they called "Rosedene" where they lived for a number of years. Herbert, a man who loved nature and the stars and recording the rainfall, got a job in the railways as a clerk in a small office on Durban station.

Here Florence had another four children: Doris Jessie who died in infancy, Hector Percy, Constance Ivy and Vera Edna. Seven year old Ivor died in 1899.

Of Florence's seven children, five survived. Four of them lived remarkable lives which we will touch on a bit later.

Sometime in 1900, after her husband, Mr Marsh died, Mary Ann Cole moved to Malvern to live with Florence and Herbert. She died in 1909 and was buried in Malvern cemetery next to Florence and Herbert's two children.

21st September 1921 - Herbert in the fields

Chapter 3

Florence's Children

Marion Eleanor (Maisie) (1888 – 1964)

Sadly, the first child, Maisie, grew up to marry Tom Lee who was not sympathetic to a highly strung young woman with German blood. At the time when Germany was at war with many countries, in Durban there was a rally against Germans. German-made goods were destroyed - German dolls and so on. And it is said that Maisie's husband taunted her by saying "the Germans are coming to catch you". Maisie who gave birth to one daughter, May Lee, unfortunately soon lost her senses of reality and was placed in a home where she did not recognize anyone that knew and loved her. May Lee was a very caring person. She never married but continued to live with her father's new wife, her stepmother.

Caption on the back "Baby May taken 1st January 1922"

May made an unfortunate decision to help an invalid friend by inviting her to stay with them. This person became incontinent and May was made to wash the sheets as she had brought her along. What is more, that friend didn't want to leave. The responsibility for getting her out of the house rested on May who had brought her in. It took Social Welfare to eventually help get her out. I heard from other sources that many people owed financial assistance to May who didn't want to be known as a donor for a person in time of need. May (who was my cousin) regularly visited my mother who she insisted on calling "Auntie Vera" though they were much the same age.

Chapter 4

Florence's Children

Evelyn Irene McLeod (1890 – 1958)

Florence next gave birth to Evelyn who grew into a beautiful girl with long dark hair and a lovely aquiline nose.

At a later stage in their married life Florence bought a tearoom in Point Road, and a lot of seamen and sailors visited it. One of them was Benjamin Orbin, a captain on a mail ship plying between Durban and Dar es Salaam. He and Evelyn met and fell in love. Evelyn even went on one boat trip to Dar es Salaam. They married, and their first child, Theodore or Teddy Orbin was born. But Ben's health was deteriorating. It was caused he said, when he was in the US navy and their ship was torpedoed during the war. He had suffered exposure and had not been able to get properly well.

1919 Evelyn's wedding day with her father Herbert   *Ben Orbin 1925*

It seemed, Florence McLeod decided, that Ben join them in the house she was building in Harrison. Made of stone it was named after the home of Mary Ann Cole's parents back in England which was Leytonstone. There was also the pun on the name as it was taking a long time to build and was late in stone. Eventually it was built and I have been there to see the remaining ruins of the house with great thick walls. Weeds and a very promising cannabis plant were intertwined with the stones. It was on a property of fifty six acres and Florence was hoping to develop it into a poultry farm.

George had retired from his job in the railways where he sorted papers in a small office high up in the building and he had bought a farm in Hammarsdale for Hector who had gone to agricultural college, though he was trained as a chemist. I remember hearing that Hector had blown up part of a laboratory with an experiment that had gone awry and I'm not sure when that was, so probably he went to agricultural college after the disaster in chemistry. Chemistry and engineering were his passions, but he did as his father wanted, and built a lovely big house on the Hammarsdale property, a farm of I think one hundred and ninety acres. Made of concrete blocks.

1922 Harrison

Ben and Teddy   *Hector, Ben and Teddy building pig sties*

Ben had however gone back to the US to see if he could get compensation for his diminished health, but he never returned to South Africa. Richard his second son was born in 1924 but Evelyn heard the sad news that Ben had died in a Seamen's Institute of dropsy in 1926. He never met Richard. Evelyn was then a widow without a pension from her husband. She was however an accomplished typist. Before meeting Ben she had worked in the railways on Durban Station doing typing work and was able to get back her old job. In between jobs she had some interesting assignments. She had been receptionist at the Waverly Hotel and had done a spell teaching typing at the convent in Durban. With modest money that she had, she bought a home in Wyebank and when the boys, who had stayed with their grandparents and gone to Cato Ridge school, were old enough they joined her in her home at Wyebank.

Richard feeding the calf

1928 Teddy and Richard *Richard and "Santoye"*

6th August 1928
Frank, Vera, Evelyn, Richard, Teddy and Hector

Richard and Teddy as young boys and young adults

Evelyn

1933 - Teddy, Richard and Baby Felicity *Richard and Grandparents Florence and Herbert*

It was a hefty walk along a straight sandy road from Wyebank Station. I wasn't very old but I do remember the house and lovely bead curtains inside the house. And what vividly stands in my mind are the peanuts that Richard dug up that grew somewhere on the property. I remember the soft sandy earth clinging to the big fat peanuts and the green leaves that produced them.

These were happy days for the boys and Evelyn but tragedy struck. There was a fire and the house burned down. Imagine Evelyn's shock at coming home by train from work on Durban Station as a typist to find her home was no longer.

The shock was too much for her. She unfortunately lost all sense of reality. I was about eight or nine and we lived in a pretty double story house in Bellair, Dickens Road, and Auntie Ev came to stay with us for a short period of time. I remember her sitting in the lounge, with some embroidery my mother had given her to do. She was very sweet but completely disorientated. She did not recognize my mother nor me or Michael. She didn't stay with us for long and was given accommodation in Fort Napier Hospital in Pietermaritzburg.

Here we visited her but it was sad that she did not recognize any of us. Richard and Teddy would have been in their late teens ... Richard was eight years older than I, and Teddy twelve or thirteen years older. Richard stayed in a boarding house in Florida Road and attended Technical College where he trained as a draughtsman and a Mechanical Engineer. At a later stage Richard did stay with us when we were in our Sarnia Road house. It was just opposite the station and he could easily catch the train though sometimes he preferred to take his car. We were most impressed as cars and telephones were not things we were used to at all. I remember cleaning Richard's car in the hope of having a ride in it.

Teddy we did not see that much of. He had become involved with Flo Johnstone whom he married. But Richard was a big part of my life. He gave me beautiful books to read from the time I was eight or nine years old and when I was seventeen he helped me buy my first car, an Austin twelve two seat convertible but we will come to that story when I write about myself as Vera's child.

Felicity, Vera, Richard, Michael and Teddy

Richard married Margaret Titlestad and we fondly called her Rusty because of her slightly ginger hair. Richard and Rusty had two children, Sandra or Sandi and Donald with red hair. Teddy had one son, Anton, whom I only met once.

The following memoirs were handwritten by Richard on the back of some correspondence from him to the Hillcrest Town Board, dated 10 May 1995. His handwriting in the notes is also uncharacteristically bad and the story ends abruptly. He passed away on 4th July 1995.

Leytonstone : Harrison Old Main Line, Natal

"Down Memory Lane"

by Richard Herbert Orbin May 1995

My earliest recollections are of my pre-school days living with my grandparents and brother Teddy at Harrison. Granny called the place "Leytonstone" which is a district of London, England joining and possibly embracing Epping Forest. I recall Granny telling me of expeditions to the forest, picnics etc. The house was of stone construction, iron roof with a wide open verandah going I think round the front and both sides. It faced Harrison Station which was probably about half a mile away and reached by a footpath fairly wide, down the hill to the station. Grandpa always an avid gardener had a large vegetable garden surrounded by trees at the back of the house. He had luxuriant cabbages (I liked to eat the raw stalks and leaves), beans, mealies, pumpkins etc. growing. Two amusing incidents I recall were with "Grandpa" having dug a furrow in which to plant mealies (maize), was sowing the seed and as soon as he walked on, intending to return and cover them in, the fowls followed and eagerly ate up the seeds.

The fowls were always 'free range' and slept in shelters at night. The other incident was, he gave me a small handful of beans to plant and not knowing I planted them all in one clump and derived much delight from the generating "forest" of bean plants – about twenty, I suppose. Another amazing incident was a snake on the one side veranda and when Granny called Grandpa to despatch it, he walked to the other side – much to her annoyance!

Uncle Hector was staying in a wood iron house on his farm "Zephyr Ridge" at Hammarsdale some 5 miles distance and I recall him coming to Harrison, visible miles away, walking through the long grass and on one occasion bringing me two empty dry battery zinc containers which he had placed over two of his fingers and wiggled them at me as he approached. I had asked for one as a souvenir!

Another incident involving the old type of torch batteries was finding a battery carbon on the path down to the station. These were black carbon sticks ±8 mm diameter and about 60 mm long. Granny was most insistent that this was a piece of dynamite and urged Ted to throw it away and I can still hear his plaintive cry saying "it's only a battery carbon".

Teddy and I on Saturdays met the train bringing my mother up from Wyebank, lower down the old main line where she lived on a small holding. On one occasion to expedite our walk down to the station, Teddy advanced the clock – but sharp-eyed "Grandpa" – who was dozing in a chair saw him - so that was the end of that!

Someone who lived with us at Harrison had a live snake collection in the one room and periodically took them out one by one, pushing their heads into a bath of water giving them a drink - so he said. I was terrified of that room!

Another lodger smoked "Officers Mess" cigarettes in yellow packets and had used to pile the packets, probably empty on the windowsill inside.

Zephyr Ridge : Hammarsdale "New" Main Line, Natal

It must have been about 1929, as I was still not at school, when we moved to Uncle Hector's home at Hammarsdale. It was a galvanized iron building lined with "knotty" pine ceiling boards. I can still visualize the ceiling as I lay in a semi darkened room (at Granny's insistence) with the measles. Hammarsdale like Jo'burg is very prone to violent electric storm and I recall thunder, lightning and hail lashing the house. I was so terrified at the noise that I tried to cry very loudly, however the noise was so intense I could not hear myself bawling, so I stopped and enjoyed the electric storm.

Shortly after our arrival, or before, Uncle Hector started building a new house some 50 m away on higher ground. It was indeed an achievement as alone, with the help of only one labourer, he handmade all the cement blocks from a homemade mould with cement and river sand collected from the "Sterk Spruit" River which went through his property in a valley probably one kilometre away. Uncle Hector's cement blocks, unlike the commercially available ones today, had very smooth surfaces as he had sifted the coarse river sand and they were laid like face bricks.

At this time a Ms Sheila Claasens lived with us as a sort of housekeeper/companion to my grandmother. She devoted a lot of her spare time to entertaining/playing with me. One day we derived considerable pleasure from drawing pictures etc., scratched on the smooth surfaces of some of the cement blocks. For this I was "given socks" by an irate Uncle Hector, but all was forgiven with "Aunty" Sheila said it had been her idea and she had helped!

Captain Purdon (retired British Merchant Marine), his wife and their five children lived on a farm, some 5 miles distance - called "Park Lea". It was a farm of ± 500 acres. He described it as 499 acres of <u>stone</u>. I first met the children, Eric and "others" standing barefooted at the Sterk Spruit River drift at the bottom of the hill to the railway station. This was the commencement of a lifelong association persisting to this day.

Every morning for about an hour, Granny taught me the "3-R's" and this I think stood me in very good stead for the forthcoming school days, as I was able to skip Class 1 and got promoted to Standard 1 after a short period in Class 2.

Cato Ridge school attendance involved a ±1 mile walk to the station each morning and catching the school train which consisted of a passenger coach attached to a goods train. Total distance was ±8 miles and the train stopped to pick up children from between the stations of Hammarsdale, Georgedale and Cato Ridge. Children came from as far as Shongweni and consisted of railway employees' children and also those of Italian nationality, who's fathers were engaged in constructing railway tunnels during the doubling of the main line. Electrification came later and all trains were hauled by steam locomotives. In those days it was one driver, one loco; and the crews took pride in their locos, trying to outdo one another.

We children each adopted a loco and the best, No 1706, was adopted by Tino Marthinus who was the senior in the school.

For a couple of years my teacher was a Miss Parkendorff (old "Parky"!) who was a lady of German extraction who took great pleasure telling us that Germany was the "Fatherland" and England the "Motherland". (I often wonder if the Parkendorff who figured in G.M.S.A is any relation). "Stick" consisted of a whack on the hand by Miss P welding a ruler, a more serious offense cuts from the Headmaster William Francis Montgomery Davis!

The shortcut from the farm to the Hammarsdale station was a walk through long grass . . . (the story ends abruptly here).

Hector's home - Zephyr Ridge

Richard and Rusty's two children were Sandra (Sandi) and Donald.

***

It seems fitting to note here that Florence always had names for her houses. Besides "Leytonstone" (late and made of stone), there was the clever name "Perseverance".

The authors collectively decided that this must have referred to the house in Point Road, as all the children, Hector Percy, Evelyn, Vera and Constance were living there, except for Maisie, and that was the only house that didn't have a name. Evelyn then followed this tradition (or perhaps it was Florence at work again) when she named her Wyebank house "Benevrith" presumably for Ben, Evelyn, Richard and Theodore.

Chapter 5

Florence's Children

Hector Percy McLeod (1901 – 1984)

Hector

The next of Florence's children was Hector. He had four sisters as he grew up. I don't know much of his early life except that he was a devoted caretaker of both Florence and Herbert in their latter years. His mother had bought a property at Harrison. And his father bought a farm for Hector in Hammarsdale where he cared for both his parents in their old age.`

Hector was brilliant at making things that worked like little windmills for us as children to hold out of the train window so that they spun and small engines that really ran on wheels. But inventing things that really worked like little steam engines and windmills didn't pay the bills.

Hector at work

As I have mentioned he studied chemistry and was employed somewhere but an experiment he was working on went wrong and he blew up part of the chemistry laboratory. This was possibly at Cedara as I recall my mother telling me that he worked in a lab which was what he always wanted to do, but was made redundant (no reason given) and after that the farm at Hammarsdale was bought for him. Perhaps the reason for his redundancy was the experiment that went wrong.

Interesting to know that Hector wrote the following in a letter to Richard and Rusty Orbin on 1st May 1977 referring to the barometer in the book "Dear Louisa" - pictured below …

The barometer was not like the one shown on page 195. It was a "FORTIN" or "MERCURIAL BAROMETER". There was a

"DRY AND WET BULB THERMOMETER" for Humidity. I broke this at Rosedene, Malvern as a small boy of 8, by putting a lighted match under the "Dry" bulb. Disaster!!

Hector in the lab at Cedara

The Hammarsdale farm was where he built a lovely big farmhouse. I remember it clearly. There was a very spacious living room with a black dresser at the back. On it were beautiful Chinese and Japanese cups and saucers.

The little tea set belonged to Florence as a child in Hong Kong. According to Vera, it was displayed in the window of their Point Road shop. People often asked to buy it but were told it was "not for sale".  Vera eventually gave it to Gwyn's daughter Kim. Gwyn still has it in safekeeping.

Hector at Zephyr Ridge – circa 1940

Grandpa Herbie

There was a very large dining room table, and Grandpa sat at the head at meal times. I was in awe of him. He had piercing blue eyes and a very large droopy white moustache that he sucked after meals. Being a small child that would have been memorable for me. There were comfortable easy chairs at one side of this large room, and a fireplace with a nice crackling fire in cold weather. Off this room was the kitchen where the cooking was done. And beyond the kitchen was the windmill. One of those windmills with blades that rotate as the wind blows. And it made a clanking noise that one could hear at night whilst one was sleeping. Just beyond the windmill was the long drop toilet that was rather smelly. Off the sitting room was a wide verandah with chairs and a couch. And inside and off the living room were bedrooms. There being no bathroom, each bedroom was equipped with a beautiful large China basin or bowl and a large China jug of water with which to freshen up. I don't know how many bedrooms there were. I slept in one that had windows facing the area where the cows were milked and where Uncle Hector, in a rondavel building, churned the cream to make butter and workers milked the cows.

Hector on the farm

I was once offered the job of milking a cow. The teat was hard and rubbery and though I pulled, no milk came out. But when the herd boy sat down to milk the cow, a plentiful stream of milk jetted out. All very interesting to me.

The milk went into big silver coloured milk cans and from about two o'clock in the morning one would hear the clanking of metal as various activities took place. This in order that the butter be made into packs and wrapped in greaseproof paper with the markings of the farm on it.

Then along came the oxen and a cart in which the silver coloured milk cans, the cream and butter were placed in to be slowly driven down the rather steep sandy road to reach Hammarsdale station. I was intrigued with the row of insects that were skewered onto the barbed wire fencing near the station by birds. I imagine Jackie Hangman? The wagon awaited the arrival of a train going to Durban, a two hour's journey away and all this produce was taken from the wagon onto the station then onto the train.

I think because Uncle Hector was on his own on Hammarsdale farm after his parents died that he liked to have Michael and me to visit when we had long holidays. This suited my mother as Gwyn was a baby and took up a lot of her time and we, as young growing preteens were ready for adventures and on Uncle Hector's farm we had them.

Hector, Felicity and Michael at Zephyr Ridge

Because he was not married and had no children, he wasn't aware of the dangers that children might encounter that, for instance, my mother, might have worried about. So we had freedom to roam as we pleased. The farm at 190 acres was big. To prevent the cows from eating the great stack of hay that Uncle Hector had stored quite near to the house, he had rigged up a split pole fence around it. At one stage when a bull chased me, I hurdled that split pole fence to land safely in the hay, with the bull, head down and steam coming from its nostrils, pawed the ground outside. I was safe as long as I stayed there.

Because it was often very hot without many trees on the grassy farm, Michael and I liked to go, with Uncle Hector, to the river for a swim. This was exciting but as I didn't have a bathing costume with me, I got creative. With some safety pins and a bathroom towel. I clipped together parts that should be closed if it were a bathing costume, and happily wore that to swim in. Uncle Hector didn't mind. He would walk with us along a narrow track between long grass and thorn trees, to reach the river, and then back to reach home. Once there was a hail storm, with huge chunks of ice dropping from the sky. The day light had almost disappeared, and walking along that track we suddenly came across cows in the mist. Quite scary for us. Uncle Hector liked us to be there...we were children but we were company. We sat together at night in the lounge next to a crackling fire, and sometimes Uncle Hector played the piano for us. This was at the time when

I called him Ninky ... I think derived from Uncle or Nunky. Out of doors it was a fun time for both Michael and me as we got to ride in the ox cart quite often. Besides the windmills he made for us Uncle Hector was making a real little steam engine that ran on railway tracks. He loved the farm animals and my father said he shouldn't have been a farmer, out to make a profit from the animals, as he liked to spend time scratching the pig's back. He also loved photography and got me interested. He possibly gave me a camera, I don't remember, but he did teach me darkroom work and how to develop my own films and to print black and white prints from them.

This skill I continued to practise back in our home at Sarnia Road when I darkened the bathroom with towels at the windows so that no light crept in, and later I became seriously interested and took courses on composition, and many finer aspects of photography. I owe a lot of my love for the outdoors and photography to my childhood years with Uncle Hector.

I must have been twelve or so when Uncle Hector took us to Frazerdale falls for a picnic and a spitting cobra spat venom into my face. I ran all the way up the cliffs to wash my face in water at the top just as a lightning storm started. A blue shaft hit the iron bridge just in front of me then came rain and hail. We walked back to the farm hardly able to see and being bombarded with hail. Uncle Hector refused to believe a snake had spat at me!

I was often at Uncle Hector's farm, often with my mother and I can remember as a child of four looking in at my grandmother who was bedridden. She was in a smaller bedroom off the end of the verandah and near to the kitchen. I don't remember much of her as she died when I was four. Before she became bedridden, I do remember her dabbing blue bags all over my face when a swarm of bees in Uncle Hector's workshop stung me unconscious. He had been planing wood and off it came in these intriguing long white curls. I thought they could improve my own brown hair and tucked them in among my long hair and then danced around the workshop with the curls bouncing. It was a lot of fun but a swarm of bees nesting below the wooden flooring didn't think so and out they came, en masse and stung me unconscious. I only remember waking up on the couch on the long verandah with Grandma dabbing blue all over the stings. I had an unconscious fear of bees ever after. Grandma died when I was four, and later Grandpa went to some retirement home where he lived another four years and died when I was eight.

Uncle Hector then sold the farm, he told me to Isaacs Geshen for their son's twenty first birthday present and today there is thriving industry there.

Uncle Hector then got a job as the Quality Control Chemist at the Amatikulu Mill in the sugar industry where they turned sugar cane into brown sugar. Brown sugar became white sugar at another refinery. I got to go inside the big industrial plant. Uncle Hector lived there at first on his own then he married Pat, a pen-friend from the UK who was the perfect partner for him. She kept a scrupulously clean house. Even the cat wasn't allowed in and slept in the coal shed.

1950's Hector and Pat

1950's Gwyn, Hector and Pat

1955 Pat and Gwyn at Brighton Beach

1955 Hector and Pat's wedding
Mary MacLeod (later Hall) bridesmaid on far left

1955 Pat and Hector's wedding

Sadly, Pat was knocked over and killed by a lorry speeding on the main road and Uncle Hector returned to his bachelor status. He was quite devastated at his loss. Later when my mother died, he bought the Hollings Road property and I became his caregiver to a degree as we lived right next door to him. He had meals with us twice a week. He had a strange both generous and parsimonious nature. He would think nothing of getting his driveway paved by professionals but would not buy new clothes for himself, and carefully turned frayed collars and stitched them by hand so that the good side showed itself. He also showed me a bottle of dishwashing liquid and told me one bottle lasted him a whole year.

He saw a lot of my children. So he was not lonely though of course he badly missed Pat. He loved photography and music, and had a big collection of music on cassettes.

At one stage he spent a short time in a mental institution. This happened when the anniversary of Pat's death occurred and he was told not to drive his car and to take his medicine. However, he changed doctors and continued to drive his car and to not take the medication. There was a guava tree just outside of his garage. When he reversed he knew he had gone far enough because the car would hit the guava tree. In guava season the fruit would fall on the car, and our family knew that he was parking. However, we did not interfere and Uncle Hector had no motor car accidents. He went on to becoming seriously ill and then we took him to a retirement home when he came out as he needed daily proper care. I lived next door but was full time teaching and had four teenagers to care for as well and could not have done his nursing. Richard came with me when he told the hospital his niece, me, would look after him. Between us we persuaded him to look in at a nice retirement home with home care facilities off Manning Road. I visited him there as did other family members. The night before he died I visited him and he told me, "I have no feeling in either of my legs." Possibly he had had a stroke. He died the following night in 1984.

Chapter 6

Florence's Children

Constance Ivy MacLeod

The next of Florence's children was **Constance Ivy McLeod.**

Constance (Connie) Ivy McLeod/MacLeod (1904 – 1995)

Mary has written a more comprehensive account which follows below but I will write what I knew of Auntie Connie.

She was three years older than my mother and held up as a shining beacon of success to me. Auntie Connie had shone at academics and from Durban Girls' High School she had won an Acutt Scholarship to enable her to go to university.

24th December 1912
Connie aged 8, Vera aged 5

Connie 1919 aged 15

She later told me it was not so glorious as there was no pocket money attached to the scholarship and where other university students could indulge in fashionable clothing, she had no such luxury. However, her attention to her studies meant she had university qualifications in French and possibly Latin. She took up teaching as a career and at about the time I was born, 1933, did an exchange year and taught in England. There she met many cousins including Donald MacLeod a second cousin.

Connie

She lived in a charming fourteenth century house called "Yew Trees" situated in Horley, Surrey. At one time it had been a laundry and the four rooms of the laundry had had their walls knocked down, so that there was this large lounge with very high ceilings. At one end there was a large beam across the width of the room on which books were stored.

Yew Trees with the books stacked on the beams

Yew Trees - Constance in the doorway

1956 Christmas Day - Yew Trees by the fire
L-R: Tom Hall later Mary's husband, Mary, Constance & Donald MacLeod, Richard

Yew Trees sign board for Constance's house (carved from a portion of an old table used by George McLeod and family at Byrne, Natal)

1956 Christmas Day - Yew Trees
L-R Constance, Donald, Mary, Tom and Richard

Richard and Constance at Yew Trees

The house had no central heating so was intensely cold in the winter except for the kitchen where an aga stove was constantly burning and kept the kitchen beautifully cosy. One had to be careful when moving from the small dining room to the kitchen that one lifted one's foot to go over a hefty wooden step at the same time ducking one's head for otherwise the solid oak beam would knock one on the head. One got used to doing this. There was a fairly steep wooden staircase to the upper level with its two or three bedrooms. I later visited Yew Trees a couple of times but going back to my childhood and what I remembered was what my mother told me.

The property had lovely big apple trees and Auntie Connie gathered these when they were ripe. She cooked with them and she stored them so that throughout the winter there were always apples to cook with.

My mother also got beautiful photos sent to her by Auntie Connie of a little girl most beautifully dressed with nice shoes and socks. Auntie Connie looked after this child, I was told. Auntie Connie played a big part in our education as she also sent us books. All kinds of books with value. In our young days it was the Arthur Ransome books about the "Swallows and Amazons" which we loved. She also sent me a lovely sewing box with needles and thread, scissors with ample space inside to store whatever item of sewing one was doing.

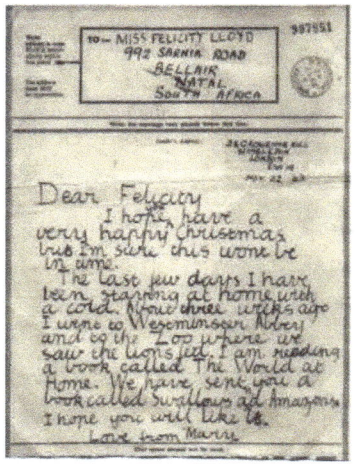

Letter from Cousin Mary to Felicity 22nd November 1943 in which she refers to the book "Swallows and Amazons" that she sent her.

 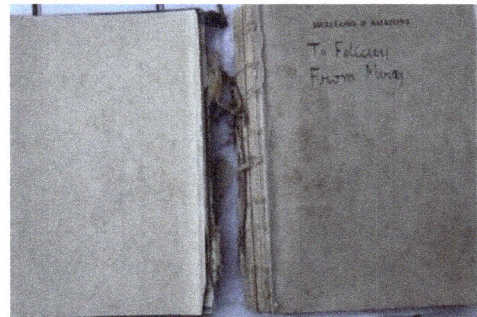

Felicity's much loved copy of "Swallows and Amazons" Gwyn has this book with her in Australia.

I clearly remember when I was about nine, my mother gathered both my brother Michael and myself close to her and told us she was sharing a secret with us that we were not to tell anyone … the little girl that Auntie Connie looked after was actually her own child, Mary. The father was her second cousin Donald MacLeod whom she had met on her earlier teaching exchange.

Donald was married to a woman nineteen years older than he who was an invalid. Connie and Donald fell in love but he refused to divorce his wife so led a complicated life with weekends with his wife and time when he could find it to spend with Auntie Connie and Mary. When his wife died he married Connie. That was when my mother told me Mary was my cousin and not to tell anyone about it. They were afraid Clem Langton might like to claim Mary as his child though Donald was her actual father.

I met Uncle Donald and he was a lovely man. I was hugely fond of him and once knitted him a bright yellow sleeveless jersey. He didn't get to wear it however as he said he would feel like a canary!

She also involved herself with local affairs and was a local councillor. She also was secretary of the Heather Society and prided herself with her knowledge of heathers. In visiting South Africa she was delighted with the heathers in the Cape that grew wild in nature. (Cape Heaths are a group of plants included in the term South African term *fynbos*).

Auntie Connie's charming fourteenth century house, Yew Trees with tiled roof had the highest hedge in Horley Row. Tall plants smiled down on other people's normally trimmed hedges. But Auntie Connie was proud of her Hornbeam hedge. Just look for the tallest hedge in the street. That's where I live, she explained.

Chapter 7

Florence's Children

More On Constance Ivy MacLeod

Written by Constance's daughter and Florence's granddaughter Mary MacLeod Hall born 5/9/1935

My mother was a complicated character. She was one of the second group of children of Herbert and Florence McLeod, having been born after the family moved from Rose Cottage, Byrne, to the Durban area. She had an older brother Hector, and a younger sister Vera, of whom she was very fond. She had two older sisters but I knew nothing about them as a child, and they will be described elsewhere. Hector I remember as the one who sent us sugar during the war when most food was rationed, and he came to stay with us in about 1946. Auntie Vee was much better known to me as a child because of the lovely letters she wrote to my mother which I liked to read, all about my cousins Felicity and Michael and later Gwyn, and the presents she sent – books, lovely handmade dresses – things she had made.

Constance was pretty, later beautiful, and clever. But with that came, I think, a feeling that she was entitled to be, or wanted to be, the best, the most important. I find the photograph of her aged about nine with Vera quite disturbing: what an adult expression for a child! She could be unkind but didn't appreciate the consequences of this.

She had no idea of empathising with other people, or the long-term affect her behaviour might have had on them.

I imagine she sailed through her schooldays always being top of the class and eventually winning the Acutt Scholarship which enabled her to go to the Natal University College in Pietermaritzburg.

Once I asked her what her childhood had been like, but all she would say was 'Connie was a clever little girl - ' but in a gardening book of hers she wrote, in shaky old-person's handwriting 'bougainvillea. Try to remember – in the old summer house after playing tennis.' That tells me that her childhood wasn't just about being clever.

Rusty Orbin gave me a notebook in which Constance had written a diary of a visit to Byrne with Hector and Vera in 1914 when she was nine, which gives a good idea of a town-child's excitement at staying on the farm.

At university she was friendly with some people who became well-known later: Alan Paton was a bit older, but he was part of their circle, and she was in love with Neville Nuttall. Sadly that didn't continue after she left, because the scholarship didn't run to a teaching course and she had to leave and self-fund the course later. A couple of photograph albums which must have been brought over to England by Hector show a happy, frivolous girl, always easy to spot because she was taller than all the other girls. The notebook referred to earlier was re-used to describe the events on the occasion of the NUC's students' train trip to Pretoria for their graduation, (she got a First) when they got up to all kinds of nonsense - - picking flowers from people's gardens - - and there are photos of this too. Later she would complain that people she had known ended up as heads of schools, principals etc., Margie Martin for example and the two mentioned already, but they didn't mess up their careers as she did hers by a disastrous marriage.

After university her happiest teaching job was at Eshowe where her good friend was Pauline Tees. After that she taught at a school in Rossburgh, Durban. While there she met Victor Evans who fell in love with her but couldn't marry her. It was Vic who suggested going on the teachers' exchange with schools in London in 1933.

I have a photo album of photos she took in England and Scotland, showing that the organisers of the scheme made sure the young teachers got an idea of what Britain was like. (One photo is of Meikleour Beech Hedge, the tallest hedge in the world, which is less than a mile from where Mary lives now!) In the holidays they were free to explore and she arranged to meet her second cousin Donald MacLeod (his grandmother and her grandfather had been brother and sister). Donald had heard she was coming through his sister Madeline who had had a letter from Opie McLeod in the Byrne Valley. Donald took her around and introduced her to various members of the MacLeod family. She was impressed.

Back home in SA she decided to live at home at Hammarsdale (or was it Harrison?) so she could help her mother who was unwell. She taught at a small school at

Inchanga but had to walk four miles each way. She had tried to do the journey by bike but fell off on a badly rutted hill and damaged her shoulder.

At this time she met and married Clement Langton, a good-looking artistic photographer, who offered her the chance of going to England again. She paid the fare for their passage in 1934 but on the boat it became obvious to both of them that they were incompatible. Donald wrote an account of this for me: it appeared that sex (though nobody would have used that word!) was distasteful to him.

In London she took lodgings she had had when she had been in London the year before. Clement gave her a typewriter and £10 and told her to earn a living with typing jobs. In desperation about what to do next she contacted Donald and he took her out to dinner, and - after a short while they fell in love and the result was me. But this was another example of how what she wanted didn't come to pass exactly as she wished: she was sure the child would be John – but I was a girl.

Thereafter Donald took responsibility for her, paying her an allowance every month so she could be independent. He arranged Connie and Clement's divorce. Donald and Connie could not marry because Donald had as a young man married a woman much older than himself (also a McLeod cousin) but he wouldn't divorce her as she had done nothing wrong. They had had no children, and now she was old, at seventy.

At this point Connie becomes Constance! No more frivolity, she had to get used to the English upper classes and become serious. But this must have been hard. She couldn't have close friendships because she couldn't tell anyone her story; it was at that time morally unacceptable. The only people in the know were Vera and a few of Donald's family who were mostly understanding. She didn't even tell her mother, Florence! The fear was that Clement might come back and claim me.

Donald arranged for her to stay while pregnant first with his sister Evelyn in Hampshire. In a letter Evelyn said how Constance seemed difficult to get to know. Later it was arranged that she would stay in a farmhouse in Devon.

Donald's sister Evelyn MacLeod in her garden at Yew Tree Cottage, Hampshire

After I was born we lived in a house in Horley, though this was not the house we lived in after the war. Donald visited when he could, continued to work in London as a solicitor, made a good vegetable garden (always did this!) I owe my love of the outdoors and nature watching to my father who walked miles with me on our holidays. And the garden of course.

Mary and her father Donald MacLeod

Mary's pedal car 1938

We stayed a couple of times with 'Pussy' (Margaret) Staight, another McLeod relative, who lived in a grand but unmodernised house near Bath (no electricity! All paraffin!) I was baptised from here in 1937.

Pussy Staight and visiting child Mary MacLeod 1938

Battlefields Bath

The war when it broke out in 1939 was the making of Donald and Constance's happy family life. As an army officer before WWI Donald was recalled to the War Office and was required to live in London, so we moved to a top flat in a Victorian house in Wimbledon. I started school before being dispatched to a convent boarding school to escape the bombing. Many children were evacuated from cities at this time. Constance took a teaching job in a small private school. I was brought back home and went to a nearby school as a day-girl. After the war was over we moved to the cottage, Yew Trees in Horley, which Fil describes so well.

All went well for many years. My mother involved herself in local things: was on a committee running the Guide Hall (I was seriously into Guiding), tested girls for Cook's Badge, made toffee apples to raise funds for a local swimming pool, took a course on public speaking, with Donald started the Heather Society and became its Secretary and Treasurer, was on the Cottage hospital management committee. She became involved in politics and was elected to the Rural District Council.

She took a cookery course hoping she could get a cooking job. There were some difficulties and Constance and Donald were estranged for a few years, but she ended this and in 1961, she and Donald went on holiday together to Essex and Suffolk where they explored relatives on his mother's side.

But he had been devastated by the unhappy years as he loved her deeply, and it affected his health, I believe, for he developed cancer and suffered a lot of pain. It was during this time that Richard and Rusty Orbin stayed at Yew Trees, which cheered him greatly. I was pregnant and still working and was reluctant to travel down from Cheshire, so I didn't see him. He died in 1964, the same year my daughter Catherine was born.

Two South African connections gave Constance pleasure some time after this. One was meeting again a cousin Mollie McLeod, a granddaughter of Ted McLeod (the baby on the Minerva) and her son Magnus, living in Kent. She and Mollie had been 'flower-girls' at Constance's sister Maisie's wedding.

*Maisie's wedding - Mollie and Connie as flower girls
Vera and Dorothy Koek in front*

The other was meeting a local man who on greeting her said 'You bear an honoured name!', meaning that in his work he had used a McLeod Gauge which had been invented by Louisa McLeod's son Herbert, a brilliant chemist and professor and FRS in England. Herbert's father Bentley III had been an elder brother of George More McLeod. See Appendix for article on Prof McLeod.

The Heather Society became her life. She was particularly proud of her collection of Cape Heaths. She made friends among the heather enthusiasts, in contact by telephone and occasional meetings in London. She took a course on book-binding and repaired many of Donald's books which were falling apart.

Our family visited in October every year, picked apples and did jobs. My son, Christopher, born in 1970, taught himself to swim in the swimming pool referred to above.

When she was eighty seven, I arranged for her to go into a care home as she had had a number of falls; none serious, but she couldn't look after herself. She would have liked me to retain the house as a base for visiting South Africans!

Katy and her partner Iain, and Chris and his partner Sandra went with me to celebrate her ninetieth birthday at the care home. Iain and Katy played (fiddle and accordion), my cousin Merle and a few others did some Scottish country dancing on the lawn.

I had cleared the house by then and took away a huge collection of papers and photographs which had to wait till 2002 before I sorted them into files and boxes.

I went to University in Leeds, Yorkshire, where I met Tom Hall who was half Scot. We married in 1959 and lived in the Manchester area. Katy (Catherine) was born in 1964, Christopher was born in 1970 after we moved to Scotland to a farmhouse in Midlothian near Edinburgh. Tom and I separated in 1982 and after working in Livingston New Town for thirteen years I moved at the same time as Katy and partner (later husband) Iain Stewart to start a backpackers' Hostel in Caputh, Perthshire.

But before starting a new stage of life I went to South Africa for three months in 1996-7 to find out where my mother came from, and had wonderful hospitality from cousin Felicity, and Sam, also from Rusty whose husband, my cousin Richard, had died not long before. I was shown around, and I did some exploring on my own in Cape Town and Pietermaritzburg, using backpackers' hostels and the Baz Bus. I met great granddaughters of George and Ellen McLeod, Jean Green in Cape Town and Althea Drummond in Pietermaritzburg and Florence (Flo) widow of Teddy Orbin. Donald McLeod had told me how to find these relatives. In Pietermaritzburg I had some lovely conversations with Dr Ruth Gordon the author of 'Dear Louisa'. A lot of what I had learned about South Africa before became real.

After running the Hostel for six years, during which time we had a visit from Magnus and Byrne McLeod and Hugh who live in England, also descended from the McLeods of Byrne, South Africa, we sold it on and I came here to the village of Meikleour, Perthshire.

Connections With South Africa.

My memories are of letters and parcels from 'Auntie Vee' and 'Uncle Hector', children's books from 'Felicity and Michael', lovely dresses made by Vera, crystallised fruit, sugar from Hector especially welcome during war-time rationing.

Hector visited after the war, later Richard and Rusty, Felicity and Les, and Vera later still.

Gwyn came to stay for several months in 1964.

When living in Midlothian we had visits from many South Africans: the Keats family, the Johnson family (in 1971), and Lesley Anne and Trevor Chorn (they saw snow for the first time and were surprised to find it was wet!)

In a 19th century cottage, I can still welcome South African guests - most recently Hilton and Yvette Keats from Texas, and before that their daughters Caitlin and Erin.

Gwyn, Wally, Kim and Ian Johnson visited us at Kirknewton, Midlothian in 1971

Kim and Wally with Ian on his back *Kim*

Gwyn and Kim   *Kim and "Scratchy-Cat"*

Chapter 8

Florence's Children

Vera Edna Lloyd (1907 - 1975)

Vera (my mother)

Vera was the youngest of Florence's children. She was not a chatty person and I didn't really get to know her well. As a child she had gone to Bulwer Road school up to Standard six when her father retired from work and they as a family went to live at Harrison, in Leytonstone, the house that Florence and Herbert had built. So Vera was taken from school and had no schooling beyond standard six. She later went to live at Hammarsdale in the house that Hector had built, where her mother and father were also living.

She told me she felt she had been buried alive, living on the farm with aging parents and Uncle Hector and no mental stimulation. To her great credit she started writing, and I have a book of cuttings of stories and writing that she had published.

This however came to a halt when older sister Connie, with the Acutt Scholarship and the Latin and French qualification read her stories. Third rate magazine rubbish, she told my mother who stopped writing.

Vera, Connie and Evelyn circa 1917

1922 Harrison Vera on a mule called Peter

Herbert and Vera *Vera*

My mother joined the local Tennis club at Cliffdale and there at the age of seventeen or eighteen she met my father, Ginger Lloyd. My father was twelve years older than she was. My father was the seventh child of nine born in East London. At the age of eleven, his father had died. In order to help his mother financially, he left school in Standard four and went to sell shoelaces in a hardware shop.

1928 Vera and Frank

1950's Vera and Frank

Vera and Gwyn

Vera and Frank

At a very early age he joined the army and at the age of nineteen he was fighting in the first World War, being stationed in East Africa. He told us stories of wild animals, of lions and leopards, and how they were not allowed to make any sound at all, no matter what dangerous animal was close at hand. My father said he was the best at sleeping in the rain. He would roll himself in his groundsheet, dig a small hollow and go sound to sleep. He contracted malaria and was discharged from the army. At a later stage he became a stoker or fireman on steam trains that travelled all over South Africa. Here he shovelled coal into the fire that keeps a steam train running. Later on, he became a Station Foreman but because Afrikaans was a necessity and he did not have that qualification, he stayed in poorly paid railway jobs all his life. My father was a kind, funny man. And by the age of twenty nine he and my mother were deeply in love but Grandma Florence was not impressed and Vera, my mother, was bundled off to Art school in Durban. I think Connie paid the monthly fees. Based on letters that she kept, it seems that she was living at Wyebank with Evelyn. She got her first job as a commercial artist before she was twenty one but immediately on turning twenty one, she and my dad got quietly married in a registry office. They lived for their first six months at the Nottingham Road Hotel until a house became available at Balgowan.

Balgowan Station

The railwaymen at Balgowan Station took great pride in their station gardens. It was the station for Michaelhouse, and where the boys used to sneak out from school at night and come down to my Dad's signal cabin where he had a coal stove and would make them cups of cocoa.

It was four years before I was born and at that time my mother was living with my father at Kloof where he was Station Foreman. He transferred shortly after to Dassenhoek for a year and then to Mariannhill for five years. After that he was Station Foreman at Bellair for about sixteen years, and the family and my mother lived first at a small rented house not far from our home at 992 Sarnia Road, then at Dickens Road in a lovely double story rented house and then for ten years at an old house opposite the Bellair railway bridge and station.

Vera 1964   *Vera and Frank 1964*

Vera and Frank 1964

Finally on retirement my father bought the Hollings Road property and they built this house which my mother designed, and moved here in 1955.

My mother had been a housewife all those years and she also had been a keen gardener, loving to grow flowers and vegetables. She loved animals and birds. And would not allow the bush on the property to be cut - bird sanctuary she called it. Even today that bush had not ever been cut. Besides animals she was skilled in many artistic forms: painting in watercolours and oils, embroidery, sewing (she made felt toys which she sold), pewter work, leather work and eventually writing again as I joined her at the Fay Goldie New Era Writing School and she had many stories and articles published in newspapers and magazines. I still have a whole handwritten adventure story she wrote for children, taking place on the wild coast and one day, I would like to have it typed and published posthumously.

My dad was devoted to my mom. He gave her his entire earnings each month and she eked these out most carefully. She sewed everything of ours, coats, sheets, dresses, and cooked lovely healthy food each day.

Pewter Trinket Box made by Vera for Mary MacLeod

Vera – early 1970's

The money just lasted though she did see we had culture in our lives. I had dancing lessons as a six year old and later learnt music when I was ten. But the money did not run to buying extras and when we moved from the beautiful rented dolls house to the very old house in Sarnia Road, the windows were tall sash type and the curtains from Dickens Road were much too short. So my mother sewed two together for each window but this embarrassed me. Funny what worries kids!

After being married to my dad, my grandmother wrote to my mother reminding her that she had a mother (she was not receiving much communication from Vera). My mom replied that time was short. She had a lot of sewing to do, hemming curtains and other things and was doing it all by hand as she had no sewing machine. So Grandma McLeod kindly bought her a sewing machine. My mother gave us the culture of books by reading to us every night. My father read the newspaper and listened to the radio. But let me get onto Gwyn now.

Gwynyth was born when I was eleven years old. My mother had forgotten how small babies are and had made her some baby clothes. They were far too big. In the nursing home was a woman who had a bruiser of baby, thirteen pounds I think and she had made clothes for her baby which were far too small. The two mothers held up their baby clothes and had a good laugh. They should have exchanged them but they didn't.

Gwyn and I have been talking about how different our upbringings were. When she was born my parents were very short of cash, now with three children, and her pram was homemade and possibly her push chair as well.

I loved this baby sister and learned to sew and to knit on her as the size of clothing didn't take long to make. I made her baby rompers, sun hats and knitted little garments for her. There was never sibling rivalry between us as there was this long age gap.

"Big Sister Little Sister"

It has always been a joke between the sisters as Gwyn, the little sister is much taller than Fil, the big sister

I had a friend with a baby brother much the same age so on Saturday mornings the two of us would go off together around Bellair each pushing a baby brother or sister. I remember Gwyn had a lovely Wendy House my mother made for her. It was interesting to watch the development of the house. My mother wasn't strong enough to saw the heavy wood so my father did the sawing. You could see the frustration on his face as he had no idea how the house would develop but my mother knew where every piece of wood was to go and soon there was this lovely big Wendy house.

My mother also created a miniature lounge suite for dolls to sit in that would go in the Wendy house. I think Gwyn had a pedal car and I do remember she said, "when my car grows up I'll give you a ride."

Gwyn and her dolls with doll's furniture made by her mother Vera

Gwyn - when my car grows up, I'll give you a ride!

In saying how different our upbringings were, when I started work, it relieved the family of the expense of one child and I paid a nominal rent to them. Then my dad retired from the railways and besides his pension he got a small job in the railways doing clerical work. He enjoyed it and so he had two incomes and their financial status was hugely improved.

Gwyn was into tennis. Dennis Slack a champion saw her as a future champion and my parents had an all-weather tennis court built at the back of their property where originally there had been a green lawn tennis court. It had a practice wall and Gwyn spent a lot of time hitting tennis balls against this wall.

Gwyn had dimples which I always wanted, and blue eyes. From my father's side as his were greeny blue. And was tall like my father.

She had a hard time with her brother Michael who used to fight with me but stopped when I went to high school and started instead on Gwyn. Dad was a pacifist and I remember him telling Gwyn. Don't answer him back. It takes two to make an argument.

My mother's three children were her treasure. Myself - Felicity, Michael and Gwynyth.

Gwynyth will tell her story first.

***

McLeod and Lloyd heights – Felicity and Michael

Chapter 9

Florence's Grandchildren

Gwynyth Wendy Johnson

(Nee Lloyd) Written By Gwynyth

I was a Tomboy. I have always loved an active life, and when I was small my earliest happy memories are of climbing trees and playing with cars and trucks in the sand, at  our Sarnia Road home. And playing cricket with Michael, and golf with my father, riding my scooter and Fil's old bike until I got my own new bike when I was six.

1947 - Michael, Felicity and Gwyn

Vera, Frank and Gwyn *Gwyn aged 5*

I had a couple of dolls but didn't really like girl's games. It was so much more fun playing running round games with the boys, cricket or rounders in the road, flying kites and building go-karts and a tree house. In fact I remember having a meltdown when I was three, stamping my foot and wailing. "WHY aren't I a boy…I WANT to be a boy…I'm going to cut my hair off and BE a boy". If only I had known that the name Gwyn was actually a Welsh boy's name, I would have been so happy. As a young child I was always planning on changing my name.

Auntie Connie introduced our family to the Arthur Ransome "Swallows and Amazons" stories, by sending his annual book, published during the 1930s and 40s to either Fil or Michael for birthday or Christmas presents. I first listened in to my Mother reading one of the stories to Michael while he had mumps, and I was about five. I was riveted - those Swallows and Amazons were my sort of children, and those outdoor adventure stories of sailing, exploring and camping, set between the wars in the English Lake District and Norfolk Broads, were to become a huge influence in my life. My Mother read them to me as bedtime stories for years. The poor darling would be hoarse and I would plead for "just one more chapter". She even constructed me a Sailing Sledge out of an old deck chair, a broomstick for a mast and an old sheet for a sail, and I remember sitting in the garden in Bellair, under my favourite Mango tree, in the height of a Durban summer, imagining a frozen lake and snow all around me, and me sailing my sledge over the ice to the North Pole.

I have read these stories over and over again, and several of the particular favourites are now just piles of pages, but extremely precious. I am still an active member of the Arthur Ransome Society, which is a literary society celebrating the life and works of AR. He was a great teacher, and his stories are for children of all ages. The average age of the Australian members is about eighty!

Cousin Richard and the Wendy House

When I was six I was in hospital with Diphtheria and when I returned home after six weeks there was a beautiful Wendy House waiting for me. Fil tells me that our Mother designed it and our puzzled Dad sawed the planks to her instructions. Richard procured the huge wooden box that provided the planking. It was a masterful construction, waterproof with a front door and proper windows that opened and shut perfectly. It was well used and moved with us to our next home in Braeside Ave, Bellair, where we lived for four years.

Braeside Ave

At this time Michael had an old wreck of a car which was aptly named "Hesperus". Our parents bought it for him as he was always fiddling with Fil's car "Shasta" while she was at work or lectures. It was green and had yellow hand prints and the words "Push here" painted on the back of it. He worked hard at fixing it up, and frequently it was "all hands on deck" as we all helped to push-start it. In return he allowed me, aged about ten, to drive the car back and forth along our curving driveway from the gate to the garage at the far end of the garden, and very patiently taught me over the years to drive until I passed my licence. "Hesperus" had a sun roof which was probably rusty and it leaked. When our father drove with him, he would hold his hat upside down on his lap because every time the car hit a bump, a shower of water would come down and he caught it in his hat!

I remember another funny incident at Braeside Ave. We had Paw Paw trees which bear their fruit right at the top of the tree, and the way to get the fruit down was to have a long pole and poke at the stem at base of the fruit to loosen it, and when the paw paw fell, you had just enough time to drop the pole and catch the falling fruit. One day my father went out to get a paw paw and wasn't quick enough with his catch, and came in grinning and laughing and with a very ripe paw paw squished on his head and juicy bright yellow flesh and pips trickling down his face and neck.

I shared a bedroom with Fil at Braeside Ave but didn't see a lot of her as she was attending university lectures at night after work, and didn't get home until after my bedtime. She was always fun and a prodigious worker and she inspired my urge to travel as soon as I could after leaving school. I remember saying "if you see something bright and fast moving, it's my sister". She invariably ran to catch the train in the morning – there was no point in wasting time just sitting at the station waiting for the train.

My father retired from work in 1955 when I was eleven, and we moved from Bellair to my parents' newly built home, "Tanglewood" in Malvern, at which time I was finally allowed to cut my hair. Another notable memory from that time is that we had our very first telephone installed.

We were all keen gardeners, and there was soon a fine garden with roses around the house, and down the bank were the vegetable garden, the fruit trees and the chicken run. I had my own radish patch and I used to rush home from school to water it and sit right there in the garden eating fresh crunchy radishes.

My father had a patent bird scarer which he made with string running from the front verandah right down the bank to the garden. At the end of the string, near the fruit trees, he attached a couple of tin cans and if he saw birds at the fruit, he would jerk the string and the cans would rattle together and chase the birds away.

Tanglewood

Tennis had become my life as a teenager, and my parents had an old tennis court, which was in our garden, hardened and resurfaced. I loved that, and as a family, we had a lot of fun playing there. There was a line of old Casuarina "Whistler" trees along the end, which used to drop their sharp, knobbly little cones on the court, and these were a hazard for me, playing barefooted.

My father always loved sport and, along with my mother, encouraged my tennis and when I was off to play a tournament he would say with a smile: "Bring home the bacon" and if I brought home the bacon in the form of a trophy, he was cock-a-hoop.

I was always keen to learn to sail, but had no opportunity until after I had finished school, and aged about eighteen, I started hanging round the Point Yacht Club in Durban on Saturday afternoons in the hope of picking up a crewing job for the afternoon races. Someone invariably needed a crew, and I filled in wherever I could. I loved sailing on Durban Bay. My future husband Wally and I were working together at Randles at the time, and it just so happened that he had become interested in sailing at about the same time, and had bought a half share in a Chinese Junk "Ying Hong", that had stopped in Durban for a couple of years, on its voyage from Hong Kong to the West Indies. I seized the opportunity of sailing with them most weekends when I was eighteen and nineteen.

1959 Lunch at the tennis court

Left to Right: Les, Fil, Rusty, Gwyn and Frank

Ying Hong

We both went to England in 1964, for eighteen months, Wally to stay with his parents in Sale Cheshire, and me to stay with cousin Mary in Hazel Grove, Cheshire about ten miles away. I worked for Geigy over the winter and travelled round Europe for a few months in the summers. We returned to Durban, married in 1966 and moved to Johannesburg and Benoni where our children Kim and Ian were born. We lived there for five years then took a sabbatical for eighteen months and built another yacht in England. This one was a 36ft Trimaran which we sailed along the English Channel and South Coast and Spain.

Then back to our beloved Durban to live in Manor Gardens, work and bring up and educate our children. We continued sailing various racing yachts, dinghies and finally windsurfers, until retirement in Australia where we bought kayaks and new bikes and for many years became Grey Nomads, caravanning and camping around Australia.

#

Wally and Gwyn on the tennis court 1965

Gwyn's wedding day 1966

1968 Vera, Frank and baby Kim

Chapter 10

Florence's Grandchildren

Michael Andrew Lloyd (1935 – 2022)

So now we get to Michael. Michael sadly passed away early in 2022, aged eighty seven. He is missed by us all.

Michael was two years younger than me.

Frank and Michael in the sea

Felicity, Vera and Michael

Michael had the problem of being left handed. In those days at school there were ink wells and pens with nibs. His left hand smudged the ink and he got into trouble for untidy work at school.

On top of that, the principal of Durban Boys' Preparatory School a very high profile boy's school, was Vic Evans. He gave Michael a place at his school, I think in Class 1 or 2 but Michael misbehaved terribly, especially in the bus going home, and at the end of the year did not make it to the next grade. He also had to leave that school and go to our local Bellair government school. The result of all this was that because he had failed a year and I had skipped a year. I was four grades higher than Michael and two years older. So at primary school level, Michael and I never really got on. I remember my parents stopping us from fighting so we decided to go down to the bottom of the property and have it out. It was physical. He pulled my long hair and I pulled his ears. And we both bawled! When I got to high school Michael and I got on better. And when we grew to adulthood we accepted each other's vast differences, I guess he liked boy pursuits like soccer and cricket and fishing, and I was not sporty though did enjoy tennis.

Michael did do well at school in the end. He went to the technical college and learnt refrigeration. He was offered a job in the United States but declined it. He became a great father to three boys and very successful at refrigeration. As we grew up we liked each other better.

Michael married Dulcie Sturgeon and they had three great sons - Brennan, Chesney and Gregory. Brennan sadly passed away on 21st November 2018.

Chapter 11

Florence's Grandchildren

Felicity Anne Morrison

Now I come to myself, Felicity.

My mother Vera and father Frank were married for four years before I was born. My dad was Station Foreman at Kloof but was transferred to Dassenhoek and was there for a year before transferring to Mariannhill as Station Foreman. The station was fairly close. The house was a substantial brick house. I can remember snatches of things. A bird falling out of a tree, dead from snake bite. Michael standing on rusty nails and badly injuring his foot. The ceiling of one room hanging low with rain water that had seeped in through the tiled roof.

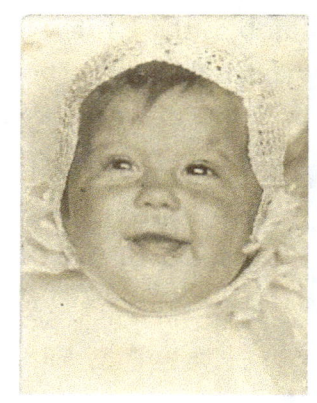

Baby Felicity August 1933

And I remember at age of six, going by train daily all by myself to Durban where I was a pupil at Chaddington Church School that took place in St Paul's just opposite the station. Some lady met me at the station and saw me across the road. The journey from Mariannhill to Durban by train took an hour. My mother had warned me not to take sweets from anyone who offered them to me.

I liked Chaddington church school and had a flawless book of work that I did with great big R's for right. I thought at that time being a teacher was a good job to have.

I also learnt dancing at Chaddington and I think that's where I learnt the dolly dance. In this dance I wore a pink taffeta dress with slim bamboo in the hem to make it stand out in a circle. And I had a little goodie on top of my head that tied beneath my chin. And we did this dance on the Durban City Hall stage. I can remember that too.

These are my most vivid memories as a child at Mariannhill except that we had a big dog called Don.

Frank and "Don"

Then my parents moved to Bellair, first to a rented house for a year then to the house in Dickens Road, and finally

back to the old house at 992 Sarnia Road. It was high on a corner plot opposite the railway bridge and that first night every time a train came across the bridge the windows rattled and I woke up. After that I never woke for any train. This was a lovely old house in which I spent the bulk of my childhood ... ten years in fact and I loved that old house. In the front were two very large bedrooms with high ceilings and big sash windows. Each of these two rooms had a glass door leading onto a verandah that ran round three sides of the house. A short passage between the two rooms led to a third bedroom and a large dining room combined with lounge. In the dining room was a large dining room table with chairs at which we sat to eat evening meals. The table was always properly set, with serviettes and the proper cutlery. My mother made sure we had good nutrition with three vegetables, yellow, white and green and a meat dish followed by a pudding or sweet dish. Michael didn't like to eat his pumpkin so my mother cut pumpkin into pieces that looked like carrots, and then he ate it as he liked carrots.

Also at supper time there was also slight tension when it came to the pudding. My mother had six pudding bowls, each with a fruit or a flower painted at the bottom. One only got to see what was at the bottom when the last bit of pudding was eaten. There was always a race for one particular dish, I think it was the one with strawberries at the bottom, and somehow even the pudding we had just eaten didn't make up for finding it wasn't my night for the strawberry bowl!

Off from the dining area was the kitchen where my mother did have an electric stove. And she also had a coal stove which was in a small scullery off the kitchen. This scullery opened out to a long covered verandah leading to the bathroom at the other end. While cold water was laid on to both the kitchen and the bathroom, there was no hot water. This my father heated for us every night in a copper geyser close to the scullery, where he lit a fire with bits of firewood to heat the water.

Below the bathroom and scullery were two more rooms one of which the owner of the house kept locked with possessions of his own. But the other room I think became cousin Richard's room when he stayed with us.

Circa 1938
Felicity at Wyebank – bird bath made by Richard

There was a butcher next door who started chopping meat at two am. And there was a large yard in which my father gardened and had chickens. He grew beautiful sweet peas and carnations and he loved his vegetable garden. He would proudly say, if all the people did what we do, grow our own vegetables and have our own fowls for eggs and chicken, they would all be better off.

A short distance from the house where there was no lighting was the outside lavatory, a small shed like building with a seat and a door that creaked. There was no such thing as toilet paper in those days, and we used newspaper cut into squares in its place. This was also what happened at Bellair Primary School where I was a student for three years, though they did have flush toilets.

It was a scary thing to go to the toilet at night. I never knew if there might be a snake inside the lavatory, and was always as quick as I could be.

For ten years, in the dark at night, I would have to leap down the sandy path to the lavatory at the back. This small shed like building had a bucket toilet that was collected once a week by the municipality who replaced it with a clean bucket. But we did have electric light, though there was no telephone and my method of transport was always by train. With my father working on the railways I could get an annual season ticket, I forget if it was free or if it was a nominal charge, but that meant I could go by train daily if I wished without paying anything.

In fact, when I went to the very occasional dance as I grew older, I went to town by train, in a long taffeta dance dress, to meet my partner on Durban station.

One such incident was when I was asked to sell tickets to the Autumn Ball taking place in the City Hall. I approached a young man who was also at university with me and asked him to buy a ticket. "Only if you come with me as my partner", he said. This was Stuart Angus Morrison or Sam whom fifty years later I married. So I would arrive by train on Durban Station, be met by my partner and be accompanied by him as we walked over to the City Hall where the autumn ball took place. Afterwards he would see me to the station where I would take the train home. Luckily the old house at 992 was just about opposite the end of the platform so I didn't have far to walk to reach my home.

Felicity (age 17) and Sam (age 21) around the time of the Autumn Ball

What was so special about this old house was that the front faced the main road with busy traffic and people walking to shop or catch the train, and the railway line and railway bridge. However the back gave an entirely different feel to life. It looked down over bushy land and banana plants to eventually reach a river. The Umbilo River I think. There were donkeys grazing there and being kids we didn't mind whose donkeys they were but wanted to ride them. They obligingly threw us off their backs.

Michael and Felicity on the beach

In that back yard was a huge old fig tree that Michael and I liked to climb. We had a nice little wooden cupboard complete with a lock in which we kept special treats like condensed milk and biscuits. I also sewed a flag, a skull and cross bones and all this was stored in the cupboard. One reached the cupboard in a place in the tree where the branches divided giving us space to sit by means of a thick rope which we climbed. You could climb the tree but the rope was more fun. Then one day we found the padlock on the cupboard wasn't sufficient to keep it safe. Someone had taken the cupboard, lock, condensed milk and flag.

Michael and I both had bicycles and I rode mine to my music lessons with Mrs Raeburn in Dickens Road. I also joined Girl Guides at age ten and became leader of the Sunflower Patrol. Our captain Stokes said I was good with difficult girls so had those kind of kids in my patrol. I loved guides and took many badges. I have mentioned somewhere the only one I failed was the cooks badge as my mother didn't like me in the kitchen so I didn't learn to cook and tried to learn it by reading what to do. I have mentioned somewhere our disaster when my friend and I had to do a cooks test and the lady in question didn't answer me properly when I asked her, is this a cup… showing her a tea cup. Yes, she said, thinking I was dumb. I used that as a measure and in the end, my custard turned out solid and my friend's blancmange was runny. Let's pour the blancmange over the custard I suggested. We got a fit of the giggles and didn't pass. Later I must have as I was given a cookery book and told to practise at home. By the time I was sixteen I had arms full of badges, all round cords and the highest guiding award, the Queens Guide award.

I also read a lot, would stay up all night until I had finished a book. In fact my mother gave me the love of books. I was about eight or nine when my mother took me into a book shop in Durban and onto the counter I poured my savings from pocket money mostly. It was twelve shillings and six pence, and that as the price of a book that I wanted. "The Long Grass Whispers", with a hard cover and beautiful illustrations inside. The author was Geraldine Elliott. I still have that book today and treasure it. African fables of the elephant who was too lazy to till or water his pumpkin seeds, and the hyena who tried to soften his voice to catch the monkey. That and other books that were popular when I was young. The William books, Milly Molly Mandy, Billy Blunt and Little Friend Susan, and the Arthur Ransome books. I remember getting five books out of the Durban library, going down to the beach and reading them all and then feeling upset when the librarian said I could only take a book out the next day as today was too quick.

Academically I did well. After six months at Chaddington church school I passed Grade 1 and then went first to Malvern Primary from Class 2 to Standard 3. In Standard 2, I spent just six months and the school put me up to Standard 3 so I virtually skipped a standard. My teacher was Miss Freeman who told me she was sorry I was transferring to Bellair school as I would have got a bursary in Standard 6, but I got one at Bellair school anyway and though I missed Malvern school and my friends there, we were living in Bellair so it made sense to walk to school rather than to go by train to Malvern. When we lived at Dickens Road, the train to Malvern school seemed the better option. I loved both my primary schools. It was during the war years and at Malvern Primary we often had a drill in case of bombs where we all had a rubber hanging around our necks and when the school alarm rang, we were all to jump down off our seats and climb under our desks and put the rubber in our mouths.

I remember too at Malvern Primary School we had a short-tempered teacher who stood no nonsense. Some boy was misbehaving so she took the hard covered book she was reading to us and threw it at him.

Her aim was not good and she missed him, but caught me on the ear. I was about nine years old and I burst into tears. Very embarrassing. But I really enjoyed my school days.

At Bellair school there was an Amatungulu hedge down the one side and at break time we made little shelters under the prickly branches and sat on the sandy soil to eat our lunch.

In those war years getting the right material for the school uniform was fairly impossible so until the war ended and we could get the right material, we were allowed to wear our ordinary clothes to school.

Bellair school recently turned one hundred and fifty years old. It is a very large school now with a prestigious hall, and my name is on their honours board in gold letters for having got that bursary in 1945.

After primary school I went to Durban Girls' High School and in matric I had an A for Botany, four B's for other subjects and one C. I got a job in the City Treasurer's Department and did a B.Com part time, finishing in the minimum time of four years. This was a really hard time in my life. I left home in the morning around six o' clock to make the early morning lecture at university, then walked to the city hall where I worked all day until finish time at 4 pm, when I walked all the way back to Berea Road where the commercial subjects were taught. I didn't buy anything to eat, as I knew supper would be waiting for me when I eventually arrived home at between nine and ten pm but I was often too tired to eat. This was such a stressful time that I couldn't fail a subject and so take longer to get my degree. I passed every subject every year. and at the end of it I became a municipal accountant. Later I took a UED teaching course and with this qualification I did seven years of teaching in primary and secondary schools. In between this I discovered writing, but that was only when I was twenty eight years old. I fell in love with it and have been in love with it ever since.

One major influence has been Fay Goldie, a Fleet Street Journalist who started the New Era School of Writing in Durban in the 1960's. I studied writing with her, taking every course she had available, and soon was published in magazines and newspapers. After a number of years as a freelance journalist, I became editor of the South African Bee Journal and this led to the writing of my first children's book, based on honeybees and called "The Wild Swarm". It was published by Tafelberg in the Cape Province in 1988. I believe it is set as a classroom reader for secondary English learners in the Western Cape Province.

Later I began to teach writing to adults and children and through this, discovered the secret of accessing the creative right side of the brain. I developed a mentorship programme, with writing clubs in deep rural areas giving children the chance to get published.

The knowledge spread and was especially helpful in rural areas where mentors trained in this knowledge could help many children to improve their reading and writing skills.... next came my interest in uplifting literacy through the creation of a non-profit company, Dancing Pencils Literacy Development Project, launched at the Hilton Hotel at my own expense in 2004. Two Ministers were present. The KZN Minister of Education the Honourable Ms Ina Cronje and the KZN Minister of Arts and Culture the Honourable Mr Narand Singh. This NPO funded mostly by my UmSinsi press has helped thousands of children to write publishable work and so improve education and literacy standards. This year child ambassadors from fifty four magisterial districts, under the office of the KZN Premier, gave dancing pencils a project to give these top young leaders a workshop in right brain writing. Trained by Ayanda Hlabisa in two very long right brain workshops, they all wrote and illustrated stories which went into an anthology called "Through the Eyes of KZN Children". This extends the ability of young ambassadors to help their peers overcome problems besetting teenagers.

My second most valuable book I have written is scheduled to launch in Jinja, Uganda in January 2023 and is called "Gum Tree Classrooms … the Power of Education". In this book I show how in one hour, using WhatsApp with video, I trained a principal and ten members of his school writing club in Jinja a city in deep rural Uganda to write publishable work. Then using Zoom I twinned a school here so that these young writers can work with rural children in Uganda and share their experiences and so grow the opportunities of both. So being a writer myself and helping others, particularly children, who grow to become adults to write publishable work easily has become my life's mission.

One comment my father used which I think inspired me to do my best was his pride in any success of mine. He would say "that's it Annsie. Bring home the bacon!"

When I was nineteen years old, I bought a motor car. My father had never wanted a car but I did. A sports car too. I had sixty pounds saved up and found advertised in the newspaper a two seat Austin tourer car with hood and dickie seat for that price.

I asked cousin Richard to come with me to check it out. He started it, kicked the tyres, checked the engine and pronounced it ok to buy. So I did and with no knowledge or

resources really I was the owner of a motor car that my father called Shasta… shasta have petrol, shasta have oil and shasta be pushed as often the battery was flat and we pushed it up and down the road outside our house. Shasta has been restored and is in good shape at just on ninety years of age. She is a member of the Vintage Car Club in Kloof, KZN. She is owned now by my son Brian who bought the car from me and who paid for my fifth "adopted" child Ivan Summerton (because for years he lived with us from sunrise to sunset) to restore it to its pristine condition. Brian says its available for fun for the family.

In talking of "family" I will next write a whole book on my personal family. From my marriage to Les Keats four children were born, each remarkable in his or her own way and all are entirely different.

Jocelyn the eldest is a perfectionist. Born in the middle of September she is married to Ross McLaren they live in Vancouver, Canada and have two children. Ashley and Brett. Brett lives in Seattle, USA.

Lesley Anne is my second child. She does wonderful work as a psychologist and lives in Simonstown, South Africa. Her two children are Mitchell living in England and Genna living in Denver, Colorado, USA. My elder son Hilton has done extremely well in life and lives with his wife Yvette in Dallas, USA. They have four remarkable children and the oldest Caitlin recently married Payne Summers.

My youngest child is Brian living in KZN. His two older sons live in Ireland and his youngest Charlie lives with him.

During my young days my brother Michael and I spent many school holidays with my second cousins, Jack and Luly Fayers who lived on Lily Glen flower farm, part of Enon farm in the Byrne Valley. I have written about them in the second section of this book, which deals briefly with the Byrne Valley, where my grandmother and grandfather met and married. So for now I will just say what a memorable time were those holidays, in a flower farm in the misty hills located on Enon farm which is part of the Byrne Valley.

Vera, Frank and Felicity 1954 Felicity's 21st

Felicity 1954

Section 2

Chapter 12

The Byrne Valley

Written by Donald McLeod in 2004

The Byrne Valley is a really beautiful place even today when the old timers say it has been ruined by excessive forestation. First-time visitors always say what a beautiful place it is. It is set among rolling hills at an elevation of 3471 ft. in the midlands of KwaZulu-Natal; Lat. S 29 Long E 14". The valley runs south, south-east for most of its length, which is about four and a half miles in total, but the lower part where "Blarney" is situated, runs more west to east. The whole area is dominated by the massive hill called by generations "The Peak", rising to 4804 ft. at the Trigonomical Beacon.

"The Peak" can be seen for miles around and if one is travelling, when "the Peak" is seen in the distance, one knows that one is back on home ground. The average rainfall was 35.89 inches (889.75 mm). It is claimed that the valley is one of the richest botanical areas in KZN with six hundred and eighty species of bulbs, corms and herbaceous plants being listed in an area of about ten thousand acres. It has been said that a special project has been undertaken at the Royal Horticultural Society's gardens at Wisley, England to cultivate some of the Byrne Valley flora.

The top of the valley is enclosed by a not too high hill covered by indigenous forest, (which was known as Watsons Bush) from which the yellowwood and stinkwood timber was cut by the Byrne settlers for building their homes. A few years ago, the Richmond Byrne and District Historical Society organized an outing to Byrne and a visit to Newborough Grange (the home of the Watson family) at the top of the valley and we were shown the remains of the old sawpits where timber was cut.

Lacking any mechanical means of transporting cut logs, a pit was dug in the area where tree-felling was taking place that was about the height of a man and wide enough to work in; the log was dragged over the pit and a long saw (about eight foot) with two handles was used, one man on top and the other in the pit. Even the planks from the cut logs were cut in this way.

How long it took two men to cut up a tree and then cut planks from the logs, I have no idea, never having seen the process. No wonder when steam power became available, the Gordon family at "Enon", who cut and sold vast amounts of timber, installed a steam engine and circular saws!

A number of small rivers and streams rise in the hills around the valley and flow south to feed the Illovo River which flows as the south-western boundary of "Blarney". The hill at the top of the valley rises sharply in the east to form the northern buttress of "the Peak", which in parts is covered in natural forest. The entire Byrne Valley is in the

Mist Belt but "the Peak" is in the Cloud Belt as whenever there are low clouds, the top of "the Peak" is covered. In recent times, the lower side of "the Peak" has been developed as a housing estate and homes have been built on a winding road that now ascends the lower slope.

Grandpa Fred said that the sea (Indian Ocean) was visible from the top of "the Peak" in clear weather. When I was young and strong, I did climb it on a fine day, with a light breeze. It was a stiff climb but well within my capability. When I arrived at the top, which was flat and quite large, I was met by a howling gale from the east which nearly blew me off. A few very upset birds did not like my presence at all and showed that in no uncertain manner that I must get off the top. There was a marvellous view but I did not see the Indian Ocean!

To continue down the valley, as it was in my day, after Newborough Grange was Dunbar, the old home of the Wally Johnson family. Next was Minerva House where the Cunningham family lived and then the Church of St Mary Magdalene Byrne, in which church yard lay all the old McLeod's and all the old Byrne settlers.

Graveyards in the grounds of the church at Byrne

Next came The Oaks of the Hoskings, now a thriving country hotel, then Etterby also a Hosking home. After that, The Gums (now Wiverton) of the Talbots, Rose Cottage of the McLeod's and later Hoskings, then quite a long way down the steep Byrne hill "Blarney", and east, lost in the forest, Enon of the Gordons, who were no relation to Dr Gordon of "Dear Louisa" and no relation of the wife of F.G.H. McLeod (Rick), second son of Fred and Opie, who was a Gordon but of another family altogether. These were farms of varying sizes, and in my day, they were farmed properly. "Blarney" was considered too hot for sheep but all the others had their flock and very lucrative they proved to be.

This was the Byrne Valley as I remember it, but with the Village of Byrne development, many more houses have been built in recent times and the valley population has increased considerably. The road has been changed too. It no longer passes "Blarney", but cuts across the hay field, crosses the river and follows the course of the river until Byrne is reached. The entire valley is now devoted to timber, except "Blarney" - the only green agricultural area in a forest which was once beautiful farm lands.

From "Blarney", the road continues to Richmond, which is set among rolling hills, but does not have the beauty and appeal of the Byrne Valley. The best times of year are spring and autumn. The summers can be very hot and the winters very cold, but nothing could be nicer than to see long grass being blown on the ridges by a strong westerly wind in the autumn.

Oh how I would like to exchange my present "home" for a patch of the Byrne Valley…

Chapter 13

Lily Glen – Jack and Luly Fayers

Written by Felicity Keats

It was through Uncle Hector that I got to know Auntie Luly and Uncle Jack Fayers. She was not my aunt but a second cousin who married a cousin so Jack was also a second cousin.

I'll start with arriving in Richmond by train to spend holidays at Lily Glen. I was about 13 and Michael 11. We had to go by overnight train to get to Richmond, now not more than an hour's car trip from here. On Durban station we got into a train that left probably after midnight and found a bunk each to sleep on. It was lovely lying on the bunk listening to the rumble of the train wheels on the railway line. When the train eventually left the station it took about two hours for it to reach Umlaas Road where we got off to await the train to Richmond. I think this train left at about eight thirty in the morning. And it took almost three hours to travel the fourteen kilometres to Richmond station. On the way it stopped to get coal or water or whatever steam engines refuel with. Michael and I sucked sweets and the winner was the one who still had a bit of sweet left by the time we arrived at Richmond station.

Here we climbed off the train, and looked forward meeting them to take us to Lily Glen. I can't remember who met us but it was an ox driven cart, with wooden seats and it was seven kilometres to reach Lily Glen. The road was untarred and the oxen quite slow. We travelled for three and a half kilometres along the road that led to Byrne then we turned off on to a track through the wattle forests that was another three and a half kilometres. The road wound up and down, the wattle trees were thick and the leaves feathery with light filtering through them, with the oxen lumbering along.

Just before Lily Glen, the road dipped and went over a culvert with small spruit running underneath then we were at the gates of Lily Glen and after another short uphill pull we had arrived.

Lily Glen belonged to a company. Jack and Luly just rented twenty five acres of it and had developed a flower farm there. While wattle forest covered most of the land, the land on Lily Glen was virgin forest. Beautiful old trees, vines and a small spruit were amongst its charms for me, along with the house itself. Lily Glen looked like a normal house but it was made of wattle and daub, in other words, the structure was of wattle poles and mud was daubed on to form the walls which were painted white. It had a thatched roof and a small dormer window as there was an upstairs loft.

The rooms were large and spacious, the sitting room being the first one with a large dining room table and a set of comfortable lounge chairs. There was no electricity. Instead, the chandelier lamp was run on paraffin and was lit each night as late as possible to conserve the paraffin. Off the large sitting room was the kitchen and pantry, a small room for packing flowers, a bathroom which had a fire to heat the water, and a number of bedrooms backing each other. There was also a ladder leading to an upstairs loft and in this Uncle Jack did photography. He had large cameras on tripods and other equipment a photographer needs.

The house was surrounded by fields of lilies. In winter and early spring it was daffodils, and narcissus, both the yellow and white kind. Then there were Snowdrops and later Tiger Lilies and Day Lilies. When the flowers were in bloom it was a marvellous sight. My contribution in return for the holiday we spent there was to help Auntie Luly in the late afternoon to pick lilies that would go by ox cart the following morning to Richmond station en route to Durban and the flower sellers and florist shops.

There was an art to picking the lilies. There was a better payment for long stems, so one put one's fingers as far down into the lily as possible, then putting pressure one carefully pulled the long stem out of its housing. It came out with a faint plop and into a bucket of water went the long stem. It was backbreaking work.

Picking the narcissus flowers was a joy as they had a powerful and wonderful fragrance. All the picked flowers went into buckets of water and into a packing room. At about two o'clock in the morning Jack and Luly were in that room packing their precious flowers into long wooden crates that went onto the ox cart and off they went to Richmond Station.

Flower farming was how they earned a living... they often spoke of cheque book farmers, not them, but others who had cheque books. But the joy that belonged to Lily Glen went far beyond what money could buy. Auntie Luly had delphinium blue eyes, rosy cheeks and a constant smile and jolly laugh. She had long grey hair which she rolled into a bun on her head and always wore dresses with long sleeves. She was energetic and happy. Auntie Luly had no fear. She had a huge belief in God and once when she was ill and couldn't get out of bed she called for the doctor. When he diagnosed her illness, I think it was bronchitis; she thanked him, paid him and sent him on his way without medication. She would get better with God's help which she did.

And the food she cooked was wonderful. She made some scones which were light and fluffy inside but had a slightly crunchy outside. Buck wheat she said. I thought she said BUG WEED and was a bit surprised as bug weed has a horrible smell. And I think is poisonous. I was relieved to hear I had misheard her.

One unusual dinner dish was porridge at night. Mealie meal porridge. I got used to it. Two incidents stand out. One was a night when I awoke with something heavy on my chest. The bedrooms were often left open as it was in those days quite safe to not lock doors. There being no electric light I had a candle and matches. And as I lay in the dark I awoke, aware of this weight on my chest. At home we had cats that often slept on me but here was only one very old cat that was unlikely to roam around sitting on people. I lay in the dark, wondering what was on my chest. When fully awake I didn't scream but just threw whatever was there off me as hard as I could, and then I lit my candle. It was a big bull frog. Seeming determined to climb back onto my chest. So I got out of bed and shooed it out of the room and shut the door.

The other entailed an adventure in another little house on the property built for a farm manager but it was at present not occupied. So my brother and I liked to explore there. It was often terribly hot, and this one particular day just outside the manager's cottage there was a pile of sticks. I moved them, and disturbed an irate cobra that stood on its tail and spewed out a jet of venom. I got such a fright that the watch on my arm stopped at that exact time. My brother and I bolted back to Lily Glen where of course it was all taken as things that occur on the farm.

Another thing we did which my mother would have not allowed was to hang a large rope over a tree and use it to swing across a large ravine. And of course swing back. The rope didn't break and we had a lovely time.

Also great fun was riding the African owned horses on the farm. These horses tripled instead of trotting, which involves a complex set of three steps instead of the usual trot or gallop. These horses did not approve of me on their backs and though we went for long rides along the wattle tracks the horses were smart enough to find low lying branches to go beneath in the hope of scooping me off their backs. At one stage one of the horses did unseat me, do a quick dance where it was and then bolt home, leaving me to walk down the hill and up the next. But it was all part of adventures we would never have had at home.

Later I will write about Uncle Jack but right now I want to take you in his van to visit blind Bentley who lived at Blarney with his wife Nellie. Bentley was blind, but must have been able to see a little as he built a water mill on the river to grind mealies and often with a span of oxen drew visitor's cars out of the mud outside the property when they got stuck after heavy rains.

I have mentioned before that Bentley was good with mechanical things and he owned a motor car. As he could not see to steer, he put his wife Nellie in front of the steering wheel and sat beside her. He did things he could manage in a car. Start it, put it into gear and change gears. Nellie steered. I hope she was also in charge of the brake. Donald McLeod, who owned the Blarney house, wrote a small book of memoirs of life at Blarney and mentioned that the village people steered clear of this two driver car when they saw it approaching.

Uncle Jack was a short powerfully built man who didn't talk much. Both he and his father were wonderful at wood carving and there were beautiful boxes on legs for sewing materials, the head boards of beds were carved and there is a beautiful carved fruit bowl that is with Gwyn.

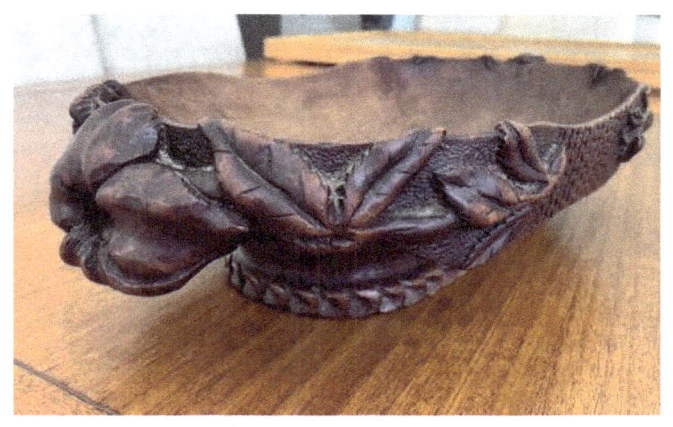

Wooden bowl with Gwyn in Australia

The Macrorie House Museum which donated its possessions to the Richmond Museum has sections of the museum devoted to the Byrne settlers. Examples of the wood carvings are in this room.

Richmond Museum

Museum Assistant

Carved sewing box now in Vancouver with Jocelyn

Uncle Jack also loved photography and I was often his model, sitting in the loft upstairs and posing for him. A second cousin Jill McLeod also was on holiday there with me once and the two of us were his models.

Indelible memories of time spent with relatives.

Family heirlooms

Jocelyn has these silver heirlooms in Canada

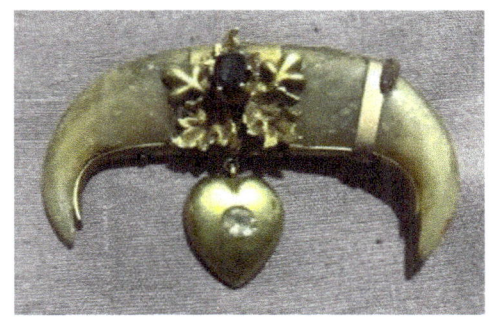

Tiger claw – history unknown

Felicity has this Chinese Locket

These heirlooms are with Sandi -

Hector's candlestick from when he was 6 years old and Florence's gold bracelet.

Candlestick made by Teddy in the shape of his profile

Katy MacLeod has this.

The bookshelf was made by Hector for Constance, from the yellowwood table that used to be at Hammarsdale. Given to Felicity in 1997.

More recent family pictures

August 2nd 1956 - Richard leaving Durban on RMS Pretoria Castle. Being seen off by Hector, Vera, Pat, Rusty, Richard's friend Tommy Morgan, Teddy, Fil, Les, Gwyn and others

1958 - Christmas Day at Hollings Road
Back: Hector & Pat, Les Keats, Mr Johnstone (Flo Orbin's father),
Donald, Vera, Constance, Dulcie, Michael
Front: Rusty, Mrs Johnstone (Flo Orbin's mother), Teddy, Flo, Gwyn

Mr Johnstone, Rusty, Flo with young Anton, Donald, Teddy, Vera and Constance

Standing: Pat and Flo Orbin
Middle: Hector, Frank, Vera, Teddy
Front: Richard, Gwyn, Felicity

1958 - Siblings Vera, Hector and Constance

1958 Picnic

1958 - Pat, Donald and Constance

Chapter 14

Blarney

Written by Felicity Keats

This picture of Blarney one of the settlers homes was painted by Jill Nicholson and is on the WALK of a small book of memories of the Byrne valley written by Donald McLeod who was the owner of Blarney and who donated it to the Museums Trust. This was in the heyday of Blarney because sadly the Museums Trust has no funds for the maintenance of the property and when we visited it several years ago, weeds and brambles barred entrance from the road. I do not know what state it is in today.

Walk from Blarney to Rose Cottage

But before that, some twenty six years ago, a party of us visited it. At that time the main house was open with a visitors book and the renovators had done their best to put on wallpaper as near to what could have been the original wallpaper. The flooring was of the original hand sawn planks with the saw marks clearly visible. At the back of the house on one of the bricks that date of the building was engraved, and next to this main house was Bentley's cottage in which we had permission to spend the weekend.

Over the Christmas weekend of the year 1996 I had two visitors from the UK. My cousin Mary from Scotland who was in this country for three months and my step son Ian Morrison from England. Ian was on a brief visit to see his father Stuart Morrison who six months previously had married me. And of course he wanted to meet his new step mother.

It so happened that I had made previous arrangements with the museums trust to allow a group of Donald McLeod's visitors to stay in the unfurnished cottage on Blarney where Blind Bentley had once lived. We would need to take all food, blow-up mattresses, personal belongings with us as well as my dog Sledge.

The walkers - from Left to Right:
Charl, Mary, Sam, Ian and Tei (front)

Ian and "Sledge"   *Sam*

Besides Ian, Sam, Mary and myself, I had with us my friend Charl and her four year old daughter Tei. We went in two cars - mine and Charl's. We were a cheerful bunch and all accepted the floor as a good place to on which to sleep.

Now the prime aim of this excursion was for Mary to walk from Blarney to Rose Cottage and maybe the Oaks.

It was a blistering hot day. Our agreement was that Charl and I remain while the group set off in two batches. Mary and Tei. And Sam and Ian. Donald McLeod was coming to show Mary around Blarney House and grounds as he had lived there when young.

The hikers had set off on the old country road now in huge disrepair with deep dongas. I don't think there were cell phones back 26 years because Charl and I had no contact with either of the groups as they disappeared into the sunset. We didn't realise what a hefty walk this was and we were concerned when neither group reappeared. Donald by that time had arrived and he said cheerfully "it's a bit like an Agatha Christie novel. They go and don't come back".

4 year old Tei

In the end Charl took her car along that rugged rutted road and found them at the Oaks enjoying a drink after that long and hot walk!

Mary Macleod Hall Remembers It As Follows:

Walk From Blarney to the Oaks 1996

Three and a half brave explorers set off at a quarter to nine to try to walk the old road which used to lead from Blarney, where Fred and Opie's farm was, as far as we had time for in the direction of The Oaks where Richard and Bessie Hosking had lived.

We were warned not to be late as our more distant cousin, Donald McLeod, who had grown up living at Blarney, would be coming to show us round the places he remembered.

Right, thought the stroppy visitor from Scotland, I've been wanting to walk this old road for ages, ever since I read the book 'Dear Louisa' in 1970 which tells of the lives the McLeods lived when they first came here in 1850. Donald or no Donald, I'm going to do it.

Fellow explorers were Sam, Felicity's husband, Ian Morrison, his son by an earlier marriage, and Tei, the four-year-old daughter of Felicity's friend Charl.

We walked and walked, sometimes on the old road, now just a track, and later on the modern road.

Sam and Ian walking along the road to the Oaks

The Oaks is now a prestigious hotel, so the road to it is good.

Tei got tired fairly quickly, though she kept her spirits up by singing. After a bit Ian and I took turns at carrying her on our backs where she went on singing - - I called her the singing rucksack. The rucksack went silent when it fell asleep for about three quarters of an hour (it got heavier then). Eventually we were 'found' by Charl in her car at about ten past twelve (we hadn't thought we were lost) and taken back to Blarney. In disgrace? My cousin was furious that we had been so discourteous as to be late for Donald! But I was unrepentant - - we had done it!

Apparently there had been references to Agatha Christie!

Donald was not upset, merely amused, delighted to show us where everything had been, conjuring up images of a drive, a top gate, rose gardens, dairying, a water mill, and at Blarney farmhouse itself which room was which, including the one where Donald and his mother Dora had lived.

Donald who had inherited Blarney had given it to be a museum about the Byrne settlers, but he still had some control over the small house next door known as Bentley's cottage, which had been built for Fred and Opie's nearly blind son. He arranged for our group, including Sledge the dog, to stay the night in it. This was fun; the whole trip was one to remember, and the story of the McLeods' lives in the Byrne Valley which we had read about was not just a story, but a place in real life.

Day at Blarney

Narrow passage at the back of Blarney House and farm shed. Young Tei got herself into several of the photographs

The dairy

Donald McLeod in Blarney House an inside view – note the wallpaper

Outside Bentley's cottage – Felicity and Sam

McLeod graves at Byrne

1996 Rose Cottage

1996 Rose Cottage garden

I now get to Donald McLeod's writing of Blarney farm. Extracts from book …….. 2004

Blarney

Chapter 15

Blarney

Written By Donald McLeod

The Grounds

The grounds surrounding "Blarney House" were extensive. The National Monuments Council estimated them to be about two and a half hectares (about five acres). As one entered from the bottom, Richmond entrance, there was a steep ramp off the main road, then one's vehicle was in "Blarney" grounds. The drive was a bit rutted but when the farm workers were not too busy, Grandpa would set them working on it so, most of the time; it was not in too bad a condition.

As one entered the gate, there was a row of pride of India trees, which were not too big, but when in flower, they put on quite a show. This was to the right between the drive and main road to Byrne. On the rather rusty boundary fence, alongside the public road, was a May hedge. When this was out in flower, it looked just like snow. This ran all the way between the bottom and top gates.

The drive climbed a short, but not-too-steep hill to a small gate of chicken-wire fence that ran all the way around the house, where the garden proper was. The first thing that caught the eye, on the left, was a huge golden shower creeper growing over a long-dead tree, and the show of yellow glory at the right time of year was just too wonderful to behold. Behind the golden shower, was a triangle of rough grass, and then came the deciduous orchard: peaches, plums, apples and an enormous apricot tree. Beyond that came the chicken-wire fence around the houses, then Bentley's cottage. Going north, there was a rather fancy garden gate with a path going straight to the front steps of "Blarney House".

On the left of the stone-bordered path was a rose garden. Growing in the middle was a flowering gum which was Grandma's pride. On the right side of the path was Grandpa's pride, the big orange tree. Orange trees are not usually big trees, but this one, planted by Grandpa, grew to an astonishing height of some thirty-odd feet! It was much photographed and prints of it were published in farming magazines and in the press.

Under the orange tree, was a little patch of fine grass which we called "the lawn". Next to "the lawn" towards the house were flower beds, bright with whatever flowers took Grandma's fancy for that year: sweet peas, phlox, petunias and any other flower which would grow, sometimes all mixed together, sometimes in separate beds. There were always fairy daisies and sweet alyssum, though, the scent of which would fill the air on warm summer evenings.

Going north along the path, which ran parallel to the house, on the left, was a jumble of bushes and creepers dominated by a yellow jasmine which seemed to be in flower all the time. Then there was a short flight of earth steps cut in a high bank, which was cut to level the ground for the house. On top of the bank was a clump of China guavas, both red and white. How I loved to pick them and eat them.

To the south-west, was a large frame covered with a Catawba grape vine. North again on a patch of rough grass, was a rondaval used by the domestics as changing/sleeping quarters. Then came a row of pompelmous trees, and the chicken-wire fence with a lot of very large daisy type plants creeping over it that were always in flower. Outside the fence was a cluster of yellow guava trees in which wayward hens were wont to roost rather than in the comparative safety of the chicken house just across the road, which went to the barn yard.

On the right of the drive was a clump of shrubs -scented verbena and heliotrope, all mixed up with a large bush of small white roses, the name of which escapes me. There was such a tangle of plants that it was necessary to go further up the drive to gain access to the orchard to the right of the drive, but when one did find a way in, the orchard was not disappointing. There were apple trees, lime trees, a few orange trees, and a mass of plum trees.

Very close to the main road's fence, under a huge avocado tree, and well-screened by the large may hedge and large daisy plants, was the "long drop" toilet. (Grandpa was careful that such a facility was never seen by the public!) Not only was it a "long drop", but a long way from the house, so far, in fact, that in later years, another one was installed a bit closer, which was well-screened by a peach tree and shrubs so as not to be visible to the public!

Near the edge of the drive were some grapefruit trees. Grapefruit was then a new sort of fruit, not grown in the Byrne area at that time. Heading north from that area, in the middle of the orchard, was a clutter of low plum tree branches and some logs, which had once been the foundation of a pineapple bed. Best of all was a large frame over which grew a Catawba grape vine. The vine had sent shoots curling around the plum tree's branches. Unless one had a ladder, it was almost impossible to get any grapes.

The only way to enter the citrus orchard was to go back to the drive, which at that point ran between two tall pine trees, which are still there today. A path led past a giant azalea bush – it must have been four metres in diameter – part of which is also still there today. In the orchard were navel orange trees, naartjie trees, some lemon trees, in between which grew yellow guava trees and odd clumps of sugar cane. Grandpa would often delight small boy visitors by saying, 'Go and cut yourself a stick of sugar cane.' If they were too small or didn't have a knife, he would detail a farm worker to cut a stalk for them.

This was the best part of the Blarney garden, with the drive on a slight curve going up to the top gate, with orange trees on the right and an avenue of pine trees on the left. I say pine, because they were a conifer type of tree, but I am not sure if they were real pines. Grandma was always singing about being under the "Blarney pines".

The farm yard and haystack were just the other side of the avenue of trees but were well-screened from view by the foliage. The drive was swept daily, and being made of hardened earth, with no pot-holes and so on, always looked just so! A good number of the avenue trees are still there. The top gate was a fancy affair made from flat bars of metal painted a sort of pink - I expect it was primer.

If a stranger to "Blarney" had entered by the top gate, he might easily have thought that he was entering the estate of some wealthy land owner, not that of a humble farmer. Everything was so elaborate. Only when the house and barn came into view would he know that "Blarney" was a farm just like all the others in the Byrne valley.

Hay Making

Grandpa always cut hay in April, when there was little chance of rain and the grass still had some moisture, but very occasionally, he made hay in March. About two weeks before the date set for the cut, the mower was taken out of the verandah of the barn where it had been stored out of the weather, and checked over by both Grandpa and the chief farm worker, who had a better mechanical knowledge than Grandpa! If any part was discovered to be worn or broken, a new part was ordered or repaired by the Richmond blacksmith. When all was ready, the night before the cut was to start, two oxen would be inspanned and the machine taken down the hay field, which was on the other side of the row of wattle trees, which acted as a wind-break for the field. (Poor Grandpa would be very upset to know that the new road to Byrne goes right through the hay field. With the embankments, there is nothing left of it.)

The old mower was a McCormac Deering, an American machine. I don't know if such machines are still used today, but with the cutter bar in the folded position, it looked like the hedge cutter I once saw cutting hedges along a country road in the U.K. It consisted of two large wheels and a central axle on which was mounted an enclosed gear-box. This, in turn, increased the speed of the short shaft, which drove a shaft at right angles by bevel gears, which by way of a crank and pitman arm, made the blade move back and forth at high speed. This is the arrangement used today on electric hedge cutters but ours was very much bigger than these. The cutter bar must have been over a metre and a half long, with hollow teeth through which the blade oscillated. The operator sat on a tin seat in the centre of the machine, with a long lever for setting the height of the cut, a short lever to put the cutter in and out of action, and a pedal which, when pressed, lifted the entire cutter-bar assembly to clear rocks.

The day before the cutting started, Grandpa would walk round the hay field of about five acres with a farm worker, who would be carrying a bundle of wattle sticks about a metre high with a piece of white cloth tied to the upper end of each stick. Wherever there was a rocky outcrop, in went a beacon. Everyone knew the location of the few rocky outcrops in the hay field, but to pinpoint them in a sea of waving tall grass was not so easy for the *"voorloper"*, the boy who led the oxen, and if a rock had made contact with the cutter bar, the results could have been catastrophic.

The next day, after the milk cart had been dispatched, the cutting would start. There was no hurry, as there is always a heavy dew in the Byrne valley in early autumn so there was a wait until the grass dried. The worker who operated the machine knew just how much to cut to fill the wagon. The field was cut lengthwise. Four or five cuts were enough for one day and as soon as the cutting was finished, the oxen were coupled to the hay rake. This was a Massey Harris, also an American make. It was a very wide machine with two big wheels and a wide "rake" with curved teeth which collected the hay. When it was full, a lever was pulled and the rake lifted, depositing the hay in a long windrow. Every available worker was called to the hay field, each with a pitch fork, to collect the hay into stocks, small beehive-shaped hay stacks, ready for the wagon. Straight after dinner, which was between noon and one p.m., the wagon was dispatched with all speed, as it was a race against time to get the wagon loaded, up to the stack yard and unloaded, all before milking time at sundown.

All the farmers in Byrne valley made hay, but the "Blarney" haystack would be the best of them all. It was, I estimate, about thirty metres long, ten metres wide and as high as a house. When the last layer of hay was put on, it was layered so that the rain would run off it, like rain off a thatched roof. The whole job of hay-making took no longer than a week. The haystack stood on a foundation of crossed poles, or rather logs, built above a shallow, wide drain. The object was to keep moisture from the hay which could go mouldy. The stack yard was fenced to prevent cows and oxen from pulling the haystack to pieces. Inside, the enclosure was kept weed- and grass-free as anything growing there could be a fire hazard if there was a runaway grassfire. On the west side of the enclosure, near the haystack, the stack yard bounded the cattle byre (an uncovered enclosure, next to the milking shed). Between the two was a hayrack, a V-shaped structure made of poles, close together on the haystack side, but with a gap between the poles on the byre side, to enable the cows and oxen, if ever they were enclosed, to pull out hay. The haystack always looked like a giant loaf of bread. When it was cut with a strange-looking implement called a "hay-knife" from the top down, the stack looked very like a loaf with half a slice cut off it. Hay was fed by way of the hay-rack all winter long, and even sometimes in summer. If the cows finished the rack, more was put in, but if they didn't eat it, they would not get more.

The Dairy

The herd would get extra feed during the winter when the grass was too rank and dry to give proper nutrition. The milking cows had a scoop of "crush", which consisted of coarse ground mealie meal with bone-meal added, and mixed with water to form a thick porridge. They were also given chafed kale, chopped pumpkin and chafed "habela" - mealies grown out of season and "stooked" wigwam-fashion before winter, and chafed to two centimetre lengths. Chopped pumpkin and chafed kale would be fed to the rest of the herd.

"Habela" reminds me of the end of winter, when all the stooks were demolished to make way for the next season's crop. When the word went around, all the little Zulu boys would appear with home-made weapons of all sorts, to hunt the rodents underneath the stooks. Among these were grey mice with white stripes which I was told made very good eating, hence the number of small boys trying to get themselves a mouse!

What still really amazes me, was that each cow knew her own stall in the milking shed. When the gate was opened there was a rush of cows but only one could get in at a time. Each cow would walk up the length of the milking shed and right into her own stall. There were approximately thirty stalls and perhaps twenty-seven cows in milk, but every cow knew her correct stall and if any cow went to the wrong stall, she was shown pretty quickly to get out by the right tenant by means of a sharp pair of horns. I am sure the modern farmer would scorn the fact that every one of Grandpa's cows and oxen had a name. Perhaps they didn't answer to that name, but nonetheless, it was so easy for a worker to say "Daisy" or "June" or whoever was limping or something, and

Grandpa would know exactly to which animal he referred.

The so-called dairy was behind the dining room, separated from the main house by a hardened earth walkway with a grape vine growing over the wall of the dining room and another growing along under the thatch of the dairy. They were marvellous-tasting grapes, not big, but with a flavour that was unique. The one growing on the wall of the dining room is still there (or it was the last time I was at "Blarney"), but I don't know if it still bears fruit. I hope so.

The dairy was so cool inside even on a very hot day. The windows had no glass but louvres, as well as no ceiling, with a gap between the top of the wall and the thatch. The first part was used as a pantry with shelves on which were stored all Grandma's jams and bottled fruit. Grandpa kept some of his more expensive tools here, wood planes, saws and so on.

Up a step, there was the dairy proper. There was a big table on which was mounted a cream separator, hooks on which the milk and cream cans were hung overnight, and of course, the butter. There was no refrigeration at all at "Blarney", but it was amazing how well things kept. Of course, cool nights, even in summer, helped, and the excellent air circulation did a wonderful job.

Burning Grass

When I travel the roads in this country and see smoke next to the road, I slow down and open the window to smell the most delightful odour in the whole wide world - that of burning veldt grass! Not only is it a smell clean and pungent but it brings back the happiest memories of my days at Blarney!

In my day, all farmers burnt grass. It was the normal thing to do, so the livestock would get new green grass the next summer. Now the conservationists say that the veldt should not be burnt every year, but say, every five years!

Like all farms, Blarney was divided into a number of paddocks, and each paddock was burnt in turn, so when the new grass shoots appeared they were given a chance to grow before the livestock were let in. Grass was burnt in August, when it was dry.

Some of the smaller paddocks were burnt by the workers in the afternoon without additional staff, but when a large area was due to be burnt, word would go out that there would be a burn on such an afternoon so long as the weather held and there was no wind. A runaway grass fire can be a very dangerous occurrence and was to be avoided at all costs.

After dinner on the allocated day, every one turned up armed with beaters and branches, the leafier the better, with the leaves tied together with a piece of green bark. The team was roughly divided into two sections, beaters and lighters. Watering cans and buckets were taken along too, just in case the fire got away. We always burnt down hill and towards the wind if at all possible, not that there would be much wind, otherwise the burn would not have taken place. When we arrived on site the lighters would collect handfuls of "zebi", dry grass lying about, and Grandpa would light the first one, and off would run the lighters along the boundary, while the beaters would beat the flames that started in the wrong direction and produce a natural fire break. The beaters would then go to all the boundaries doing the same thing.

A grass fire is a spectacular sight with clouds of grey smoke and leaping flames some twelve feet high or more, with birds flying through the smoke to catch any insect that flew up from the flames, and the occasional rabbit or small buck trying to escape the fire! And the wonderful smell of burnt grassland!

When the burn was finished, Grandpa was very conscious that everything must be left in order with no burning tree stumps that could flare up with a wind and ignite something to start a fire in dry grass somewhere. A grass fire that gets onto the next farm can be a very serious matter and I was often dispatched to look at such and such a place to see that there was nothing smouldering there.

It was during a burn of a paddock close to the house that I met, when I was still a small boy, the only other brother of Grandpa Fred, that I had met other than Herbert (Herbie) who came to Blarney every year for some time for his holidays. The burn was near the main road and a passing car stopped and an old man with a white beard got out, scrambled up the bank and greeted Grandpa with "Hello, Fred. Nice to see you". And I was introduced to Uncle Frank. Grandpa Fred had a white beard but it was cut short and trimmed, while Uncle Frank had a big white beard, and looked very venerable.

The Trees and Animals

When I think of Blarney, I think of trees. In my time there were trees everywhere. Not only fruit trees, but oak trees, wattle trees and gum trees as well as a few not so well-known trees. A walnut tree, a loquat tree and two pomegranate trees, which I well remember with their shiny dark green leaves and big red fruit which is not really edible but very nice to break open with hard red seeds inside.

There were oaks everywhere, some of which are still there. The big trees have gone but the small trees in my day have now become big trees. And there were gum trees a-plenty. To the west of the house was a forest of gums planted as a windbreak, in a semicircle. They were big trees with a trunk a good half-metre in diameter, and about thirty metres in height, in which hadeda ibis and black crows built their nests. The windbreak was fifty or sixty metres long and it needed to be, as the cold west wind swept down the opposite hill, and without the "forest", the house would have been very bleak. The oak trees were everywhere. There was a big one just off the back yard outside the "Pack House" with an anvil and grindstone under it. There was another outside the workshop as well as two big ones to the southwest under which the washing was done. (This was accomplished using an outside fire, three-legged pots and old fashioned hand-cranked washing machine.) How wonderful it was in the spring when all the oaks were out in new leaf.

The forest of wattle trees across the main road provided us with firewood and a row of wattles on the west of the "near land" acted as a windbreak for the crops. There were even some indigenous trees in the open grassland, which provided shelter for the livestock, as well as the "bush" as we called it, a patch of indigenous forest growing on a steep hillside in which, I expect, resided buck and rabbits.

Farm animals, we had aplenty, but there were no sheep or horses. "Blarney" was too hot for sheep and Grandpa Fred's theory was that horses cropped the grass too short so there was not enough for his beloved cows! The cows, in my time, were Ayrshires, before he tried Gurnseys, but the Ayrshires were better for milk production. He could not stand pigs or goats so there were none of those. The "count" as it was called, was about sixty cows, oxen and "tollies" (bullocks), but this figure did not include calves which numbered about twenty at any one time, and also two old mules for the milk cart. Just about right for a four-hundred-and-ten acre farm, which was small for the Byrne Valley.

Chickens we had, though how many in all I am not too sure. About forty, I would say. Geese were tried at one time but proved too dangerous. There was a very good flock of turkeys but they were dropped for a reason I do not know.

Chapter 16

Blarney Farm

Written By Donald McLeod

"Blarney Farm" was a working farm like all the other farms in the Byrne Valley, meaning that it had to make an income for the owner, who was, in this case, Grandpa Fred. What the income from "Blarney Farm" was I have no idea. Wonderful man that Grandpa Fred was, record keeping was not his strong point, except for milk production which was recorded every day. No records were kept. I did see a very crude entry once that stated that he had sold so many bags of mealies, and the cost of fertilizer, but that was all!

What made the small income go so far was the fact that we were almost self-sufficient. We grew everything we needed so there was no need to buy anything other than a joint of meat twice a week, flour, yeast, sugar, salt, pepper, matches, candles, paraffin, and at Christmas time, a packet of spices for cake making. And I suppose clothing sometimes, but otherwise, everything was there.

There were five fields used for the planting of crops, which Grandpa called "lands" - the "near land", the "low land", the "spring land", "Emily's land", and the "top land". In later years, the latter two were turned into pastures and not used for agriculture. The "near land" and the "low land" were the most productive. The "near land" must have been at least ten acres in extent which was the main maize and potato-growing area. As it was visible from the main road, the rows of maize or potatoes had to be straight and a great deal of trouble was taken to get the first row straight. If the planter followed the first row on all the succeeding rows, Grandpa was happy!

All the farm produce was sold at such a low price that I wonder how we could come out, but we did. I was never hungry or cold or wet and I am sure the rest of the family was the same. We were happy with simple things. To think back at the price farm produce sold at amazes me. A two hundred pound bag of mealies sold for one pound (R2-00) a large pumpkin for one shilling (10c) or perhaps a very large one for 1/6p (15c). A chicken if we sold one was 2/6p (25c); the milk was considered of such value. Quota milk (the dairy gave us a quota of so many gallons a day) was about seven pence a gallon. Surplus milk brought in about four pence a gallon! We sent off each day, except Sunday, about twenty gallons. The rail charges had to be deducted from the monthly cheque from the dairy.

The "Blarney" pumpkins were marvellous, some Cinderella-shaped, some round and flat, some just round, all golden yellow with a green flake, and orange inside, with the most marvellous taste, no matter if boiled, baked with the joint or made into fritters. We stored them on the roof of the Barn or wherever there was shade and they kept for nearly a year. (I saw a large pumpkin in a fruit and veg shop the other day. It was a big pumpkin but it was priced at R55-00! I could not believe it!)

The potatoes were just as good never exposed to the sun and floury when cooked. Early on, Grandpa grew "flowerball" potatoes but switched to "up to date" later, a large potato with a slightly grey skin. In order to get a good crop, he would order two boxes of seed potatoes from Scotland every year! And apart from this, we grew kale, a sort of large cabbage, for cattle winter feed. And, of course, maize.

Nothing smelt nicer than when walking in a mealie field with the plants shoulder-high and young fresh leaves. In between them, were pumpkin vines with very small pumpkins, ready to grow into big "Blarney" pumpkins! Life was very pleasant at that time.

Blarney - Grandpa Fred

Grandpa Fred was a truly remarkable man. As far as I am aware he had no formal education whatsoever. Grandma Opie went to St. Mary's School in Richmond. When Grandpa was young, he was a herd boy, and after that, he became a transport rider taking goods from 'Maritzburg to the Witwatersrand, and even as far as Barberton, in what is now Mpumulanga Province. He was not a country bumpkin, however. He could talk on any subject and had a very good knowledge of politics, both local and U.K. politics. The only thing he had very little knowledge of was mechanics. He left all that to his son, Bentley, and when Bentley left "Blarney", he relied on me. Neither he nor Grandma ever learnt to drive a car, although during World War 1 there were plenty of women driving cars.

Grandma was nine years younger than Grandpa. They never had a telephone installed at "Blarney", but the lines to Byrne went past both the top and bottom gates.

Fred and Opie

Grandpa's day would begin at four a.m. every day. His first job was to clean the kitchen stove grate and light the fire which burned all day long. He would fill two big kettles and put them on so that there would be hot water when Grandma rose about an hour later. When Grandpa went out at about half past four in the morning, he had to carry a hurricane lantern, even in summer. He went over to the cow shed to get the herd in and fed before the milking at first light. Breakfast was at seven o'clock, then the milk cart was dispatched after the milk had been cooled and weighed.

Then farming operations would begin. Wherever the workers were, Grandpa was there, supervising. Satisfied, he would move on to another field to see what needed to be done. All of this was done with the aid of two sticks. Even at the age of seventy-five, he got along at amazing speed, but he did avoid the very steep areas at "Blarney". At a quarter to twelve, he would shout to the workers that it was dinnertime, and the bell was rung at twelve noon. After he had had dinner, the bell was rung again at one p.m., to indicate the dinner hour was over, and he would then go and have a nap before going out again.

The cows were stalled and fed in the late afternoon, ready for milking at sunset. After the milk had been separated with the aid of a hand-cranked separator, the workers would go home and we would all go to tea (we still used the Scottish name for the evening meal), after which Grandpa and Grandma settled in their rockers on either side of the fireplace in the sitting room. If it was winter or wet weather, there would a fire in the grate, but in summer there was no fire. We would read by the light of a paraffin lamp until nine o'clock which was bedtime. I was accustomed to reading by the light of a single candle.

What was so nice back then was that there was no violence or crime. Of course, we had the odd chicken stolen at night and a few mealies stolen, but everyone was respected. If indigenous people wanted to cross the farm, they would come and ask permission. It was a law-abiding country then and a law-abiding world.

One thing that was not so nice about "Blarney" was the perennial shortage of water. There was a rainwater tank at each corner of the house, in some places, two, one feeding into the second when full, but the main source of domestic water was a small spring at the bottom of a very small slope of about two hundred metres. The water was fed into a covered reservoir of about five by three metres and perhaps about one metre at its deepest point. This gave a head of water to operate the contrivance known as a hydraulic ram. This was very popular with farmers before electricity became available nationwide. I have never really understood the principle on which it worked. The drawback was that it wasted three-quarters of the water supply while pumping one quarter, which it did very well in spite of the lift required. The ram fed one tank and then a second. Someone had to go every evening to turn it off, to allow the reservoir to fill and then go the next morning to start it up again. Ma, Grandma, the house girl or I had to do this every day.

When Bentley left "Blarney", the lot fell to me to maintain this piece of machinery, and many times, I spent the entire afternoon working with the head farm worker, who had a sound mechanical knowledge, stripping, cleaning and reassembling. We usually got the beast working again, but if parts were worn, I had to get Grandma to order spares from Pietermaritzburg, which took a couple of weeks to come. Meanwhile, we had to rely on rainwater.

Another installation at "Blarney" which proved to be extremely reliable was the water-driven mill on the river, always referred to as "Bentley's Mill". It was very well engineered and installed. When he was young, as he was so strong, Bentley was pressed into grinding mealies with a hand-cranked mill, a job which he very much disliked. He installed a water-driven mill, and the story was that he had dug the entire mill stream (the canal which fed water to the mill) on his own, single-handed, a contention which I took with a big pinch of salt. The canal was on average one metre wide and was from one and a half metres to over three metres deep and at least one kilometre long. There was also a question of levels. He would not have known if it was too deep in places and too shallow in others. The mill stream started from a rough dam across the river, which diverted some water. Near the mill house, there was a T-junction, which allowed water to return to the river when the mill was not in use. This was blocked off with a sluice gate, which was made of battened planks in concrete guides. With the waste gate closed, the water flowed in a wooden trough over the abyss to the enormous wheel which was located in a large pit. (It is still there today.) After the wheel, the water flowed back to the river by way of a tailrace. Belting taken through a hole in the floor drove a counter shaft, which in turn drove the mill. The high speed needed was obtained by the ratio on the pulleys, plus the gearing on the mill.

We ground four types of meal: very coarse crush for chicken feed, finer for cattle feed: fine for the workers and very fine for domestic use. The quantity used was amazing. We milled every two weeks and it would take the entire afternoon. The next day, it was all brought up to the barn by ox wagon for storage in the barn. The mill was very well engineered and installed. The mill house itself was rather patchy, but was weather-tight by necessity for the storage of mealies.

Grandpa hated machinery, and anything which had a handle had to be cranked by hand rather than driven by power. So when Grandpa went to live at Wiverton with Uncle Archie, I told Mum that I could convert the sheller to be power-driven. She laughed at me and said I would never do it. But I proved I could. (I was about seventeen at the time). With the help of the head farm worker, we turned the sheller around, and bolted it to the floor. Amazingly, there were two bolts concreted in just the right place. We found a length of unused belting, which only needed slipping into place and we were ready for the test. Somehow, I had not calculated the speed of the water wheel correctly, not taking into account that the load on the mill was very high, while on the sheller, was slight. Anyway, at the first attempt, the sheller nearly jumped off the bolts it was going so fast. But with a bit of trial and error at the sluice gate, we found just the right setting that would allow the sheller to run at the correct speed, and from then on, shelling was a pleasure. Mama just could not believe that I had got it right! But we only had one season before Grandpa died mid-1939 and Bentley returned to "Blarney", so instead of being a farmer, I spent my working life working in a mechanical capacity.

There were always farming operations to attend to: ploughing, planting, weeding, earthing up potatoes, haymaking, getting and sending goods to Richmond, which lies about seven kilometres south of "Blarney", accessible on a very rough road. (There were no tar roads back then). The going was sometimes impossible after it had rained.

Grandpa Fred was a very kind-hearted man as was proved again and again when motorists, new to country driving in muddy conditions, got stuck on the Byrne hill. Very few, if any, town drivers knew of or fitted mud-chains on their tyres, as all the local motorists did when the conditions became slippery. And many a driver, having got himself and his family stuck in the ditch as he started to climb the hill, which went past "Blarney", called on Grandpa for assistance.

It always seemed to rain during a holiday season, Christmas or Easter, and the over-confident driver, having driven on nearly flat roads since leaving the tar, would arrive at the Byrne hill, and find the car wheels would lose their grip and the vehicle would drift sideways. A good driver would have eased up on the throttle to get a better grip, but the town driver invariably did just the opposite. The wheels would spin on the muddy greasy surface and the car would land in the ditch at the side of the road, which all country roads had at that time. The more the driver would try to get out of the ditch, the more he would be stuck. Seeing a farm house, the exasperated driver, realizing that a tow was the only solution, would soon be banging on the front door, not caring if the farmer had just knocked off for the day after a hard day's work. Some even came at ten o'clock at night so poor Grandpa had to shout a to the workers to inspan the oxen even if he had to go all the way to the nearest workers hut to get the staff together, and he himself would go out in the rain and mud to supervise the tow.

After "Blarney" house, the hill flattened out a little and the road surface was harder, which gave it more grips, so the vehicle was towed there, where there was a chance that the rest of the journey would be completed.

It even happened twice one Saturday afternoon. Just as Grandpa had completed one tow, and had outspanned the oxen, another man arrived to request assistance. And when the stranded motorist offered to pay, which most did, dear Grandpa refused to take anything! What a kind-hearted man he was.

The stranded motorists were usually on their way to visit relations or friends in the Byrne Valley or even further, or to stay at the "Oaks", which even in those far-off days was a sort of country hotel.

After this time, the road was hardened, gravel chips being rolled into the surface which was an improvement, but when the road was tarred many years later, the "Blarney" hill was cut out and the road re-routed to cross the river down-stream from the mill and followed the course of the river. The old road is still there but only used by the forestry company as an excess route when timber is felled.

Chapter 17

Donald McLeod's Life at Blarney

Written By Donald McLeod

The temperature at Blarney varied widely, and, I suppose, still does. In summer, it could be as hot as blazes, but with no humidity at all. In winter, it was as cold as could be. I'll give an indication of just how cold it got once. By the chicken run was a large stone mortar. Where it came from I have no idea. It was used as a drinking trough for the chickens. Chickens stand on anything which contains food or drink, and if it is light in weight, it will tip it over, so this heavy mortar was used. One winter's day, Grandma went to fill up the mortar and found ice on top. Tipping it over, she discovered that the ice went all the way to the bottom. In other words, the mortar which was about twenty-four cm deep and twenty centimetres in diameter was solid ice at eleven a.m. on a sunny day!

I wore very little clothing, winter or summer. I wore shoes, usually the *veltskoon* type, socks, British Army-type shorts, an under-vest, a shirt, a floppy hat in the sun and perhaps a light jersey, but I never felt cold, even with frost white on the ground. What, I suppose, kept me warm was that anywhere I went, I went at a run, downhill, full speed, on the level, at a fast trot. The only time I walked was when I went up hill. The sheer exuberance of life gave me all the energy I needed. But I had some nasty illnesses when I was young, though I always seemed to come out on top. Grandpa and I always got 'flu in the winter. The other family members only got it sometimes, but poor old Grandpa and I got it really badly. In those days, there were no antibiotics or suphanilamide drugs. The only treatment known to the local doctor was aspirin, to which I was allergic. For a few days, I would live on grapefruit juice and water. At times, I was forced to drink the most horrible-tasting drink "Benger's food", a powder mixed with hot milk. The very thought of it makes me shudder. If the manufacturers had added some sort of flavour, perhaps it would not have been so revolting. Another product that I was goaded to drink was "Allenbury's Diet". This was also mixed with hot milk, which I can't stand. This was not quite as bad but still pretty awful.

The Workshop

It was after recovering from one of the attacks of 'flu that I had a happy surprise. It was my first day out of bed and I was feeling pretty shaky. Ma said, "Come and look", and there, built as a lean-to against the wall of the pack house was a dinky little workshop built by Grandpa for me! I was always keen on using tools and had a few, but found the benches in the pack house too big and high and the vices too clumsy for me to be able to use them. (The pack house was so named because all the fruit was packed for sale there. It was made of clapboard, open at one end, garage-style, with heavy benches on each side. All the hoes, spades, rakes and so on, were kept there, as well as Grandpa's hand tools.)

My little shop was so made that I could stand up (as I got taller, they dug the floor down). It had a little bench the right height, and a delightful little vice. I was so happy; here was somewhere I could work. The roof, I think, was thatched, the walls were just small poles covered with "Malthoid", a sheet type of roofing which was very popular at the time. It was fitted with a strong wooden door. I was *so* happy! About the same time, Ma gave me a book which I still have (now without a cover), called "The Boy Electrician" and I was wont to carry out the experiments contained therein when the weather was wet or too windy to go out of doors.

The women at "Blarney"

During my years at Blarney there were only three women: Bentley's wife, my mother and Grandma.

Bentley's wife was a strange woman indeed. She had been a town dweller and seemed to resent living in the country. However, in the early 1930's she and Bentley left to live on the South Coast.

My own mother was a wonderful mother to me and I am forever grateful to have had a mother like her.

Grandma Opie (Sophia) was a Talbot and of Irish descent and was full of fun in spite of being old when she was still quite young. She was short and very bent, with lots of lines and wrinkles in her face. She was nine years younger than Grandpa but he looked much younger in spite of his white beard. He still had very blue eyes and a pink complexion. Grandma died first, in 1936, while Grandpa lived until 1939. Grandma was a marvellous housewife. Everything had to be clean and well-run, and she was not afraid of hard work. And she was a wonderful cook: bread, cakes, tarts, both big and small, and puddings of all sorts, came out of Grandma's kitchen. Stewed fruit and jam and marmalade were made whenever fruit was available.

Before they settled at Blarney, Grandpa and Grandma went transport riding together. Grandma told me that they slept under the wagon at night, and how hard it was to get a fire burning when the brushwood was wet! Can you imagine a modern bride living in such conditions?

The Cats

When writing of "Blarney" in the old days, I must mention the cats. I have always loved cats and it could have been the "Blarney" cats which led me to like them so. Dogs, I do not like, and never have, and there were no dogs at "Blarney". Grandpa kept an army of cats to keep down the rat population. As well as that, we had domestic cats, the best of which was Ma's big grey neutered tomcat, a very big cat that lived for sixteen years. Wherever Ma moved to (and she had quite a few moves) Pam always went too. Why he delighted in the name of Pam I just don't know. He was so big, he took up a whole chair.

There was no space to share with Pam. Grandpa would come in and say, "What a lux-u-r-i-o-u-s cat!"

At least three times a week someone would say, "Let's go for a walk to the top gate." It was a nice easy grade, nice surface, among beautiful trees and not too far. Pam would, of course, come too. Half-way up he would disappear into the orange orchard. He would wait until we came back then he would pounce out at us from behind a tree with fur fluffed up, looking even bigger than he really was, just to give us a fright. Of the barn cats, I knew very little, except there were quite a few. Grandpa Fred loved the barn cats and every morning after breakfast, he would be seen with a billy can with left-over porridge mixed with milk, feeding his cats! I once counted the entire cat population at "Blarney" and I think that there were ten or twelve cats in total.

Richmond

All the household supplies came from Richmond. The few things we needed came from the butcher, the grocer and the pharmacist. Soft goods were sold in the grocer's shop at a counter across the shop from the grocer, and sold by a different shop owner – two businesses in the same shop! There was also the hardware merchant together with the blacksmith, one motor repair garage and one filling pump operated by the general merchant store, of which there were a number, all run by Indians. There was a railway station and a large steam-driven sawmill, with an "on" and "off" hooter which could be heard at "Blarney" when the wind was right. Electric mains came to Richmond about the mid-1930s and there was great excitement as the street lights were switched on, which, we at "Blarney" could see clearly. About this time, the National Road to the Cape was built on or very near the existing road to Pietermaritzburg. This was just an earth road, but the National Road was first gravel and then tarred. It was many years later that the tar was extended to Byrne Valley. Electricity came too. There are mains at "Blarney", but not in the main house, as this would spoil its historic value. Richmond, some sixty years later, is not much different to what it was back then. Howick, on the other hand, being much closer to Pietermaritzburg, has gone ahead with two large retirement villages and some light industries.

One man that I was not too happy to see was the Richmond doctor, the District Surgeon. I well remember feeling pretty sick on many occasions and Dr. Mackintosh peering at me through thin gold-rimmed round spectacles hooked well behind his ears. He had thin sandy hair and a sandy moustache and he smelled of a chemical odour that all doctors and hospitals seemed to smell of at that time (but which now, for some unknown reason, is not evident on medical personnel or in establishments).

The Top Gate

All this reminds me of an incident which happened when I was perhaps seven or eight years old. I was quite capable of going all around "Blarney" by myself. We were all gathered in the sitting room after tea (supper). I think that there were more than just the normal family, perhaps there were some evening visitors, or more likely, people staying as house guests. Someone remarked what a beautiful evening it was, with no wind, a full moon and no clouds. (It was long before the days of pollution.)

Grandpa must have been in a playful mood. He said, "Donald, if you go up to the top gate, I will give you ten shillings." Ten shillings was a lot of money to me at the time so I did not say no, but I felt a bit uneasy. I had never liked going to the top gate much. It was a lonely sort of place with the house being out of sight, especially if there were no farm workers about and no traffic on the road. The wind moaned through the top branches of the pine trees. Now, if Grandpa had said go over to the barn or even to the "near land" (the nearest field), I would have jumped at it, but the top gate! Then a discussion took place as to how they could be sure that I had really gone to the top gate. The last pine tree in the avenue had pine needles, with not the type the other trees had, so I was told to bring back a twig of the needles from it.

The length of the drive from the house to the top gate must have been at least two hundred and fifty metres, and about fifty metres up were the two big pines which met overhead. In these trees resided a number of spotted eagle owls, big birds about forty three centimetres in length, whose mournful "Vooo hoo" could be heard very clearly from the house. I was told to put a jersey on as it was cold. This I did then I went out of the front door along the verandah, up the earth steps past the China guava trees and out into the drive from the small gate. The moon was so bright that everything looked white except the shadows which were black. I walked up the drive into the deep shadow of the big pine trees and just in the centre of the shadow, an eagle owl above my head called, "Vooo hoo". I should have known that it was just an owl, but I turned and ran back to the house as fast as I could. I crept in by way of the back door and went back to where I had been sitting. No one took any notice. Thankfully, the conversation subject had changed and no one seemed to remember about me going to the top gate! Grandpa must have known his money would be safe.

The House and Outbuildings

"Blarney House" was built of a home-made and fired brick: It has been said that the bricks are green bricks, meaning not fired, but I know for a fact that Grandpa Fred burnt all his bricks. The clay from which they were made was a light-yellow colour. They gave the house that wonderful light golden glow, which was spoilt by some of the bricks being over-fired and dark brown.

The house was built by Grandpa Fred for Grandma Opie, whom he married on the 28th October 1878, and it was the home they lived in for the whole of their married lives. It started off as a two-roomed cottage with a small kitchen attached to the back and a brick-paved verandah in front with a trellis. As the family grew, more rooms were added on, and now the house is a seven-roomed house, plus bathroom and kitchen, with an outside dairy. But the National Monuments Council refer to it as the "Blarney Settler Cottage". The last addition was a dining room and kitchen at the back and the dairy. Being built piecemeal meant that most rooms are not on the same level, which meant a step up or down, which could be very awkward at times. There was no running water in any room. A pipe from the ram-fed tank at the top of the grounds supplied a tap just outside the kitchen door, water from which was used for cooking, washing-up, washing of hands and the bathroom.

The back verandah was slasto (crazy paving) and all the steps were stone or brick. The roof was galvanized iron, painted red, and the wonderful thing is that when the building was being restored as a national monument, the roof was found to be in a very good condition after a period of at least sixty years, perhaps more, as the roof had never been repaired during my time at "Blarney" and certainly was not repaired after that! The fact was that when "Blarney" was built, things were made to last, not like today! The original roof may have been thatch as I am not sure if corrugated iron was obtainable in 1878.

From the back yard of "Blarney House" looking north-west, the first building that could be seen was the pack house, after that the chopping block and trestles for cutting and chopping firewood. We burnt an amazing quantity of firewood, and every day except at the weekend, someone had to cut and split firewood. The sound of a saw and axe were part of the "Blarney" sounds, the same as hens cackling and cows mooing. Then inside the staff house, or just outside, a fire would be burning all the time, cooking the staff meals. After an enormous pile of uncut firewood came the farm yard and then about one hundred metres from the house was the barn, which is still standing today, built half of brick and half of timber. The bricks here were brick red, not the same as the house bricks. At one end of the barn was a lean-to used as a wagon shed, and at the other end, was a stable which was used when there were horses. In my day, there were only a couple of mules. The barn itself consisted of two rooms with a covered verandah, in which were stored agricultural implements of every description, as well as two one thousand gallon grain (mealie) tanks. Inside the barn, when the stable-type door was opened, the first thing that was likely to be seen was one or two cats sleeping on a sack, tired out after the night mouse-patrol!

Two one thousand-gallon mealie tanks were on the left, and on the right, two large yellowwood bins for crushed animal feed, and to the right, a door that led in to the second room, which was a potato store. Potatoes cannot be exposed to the light for long otherwise they turn green, so this room was very dark with a slatted floor standing on beams for ventilation. A number of bricks were left out of the walls for the same reason. If one went in after being in the bright sunlight, one could see nothing, but after a few minutes, the potatoes could be seen spread out on the floor, not more than one layer deep, and if there was a worker who was not too busy, he would be sent in to turn over the potatoes.

The big mealie tanks also had to be cleaned out when the last of the contents were drained out. At the bottom, instead of a tap, as a water tank would have, there was a short twelve centimetre diameter pipe with a cover, which, when removed, allowed the mealies to run out into a sack or some sort of receptacle. A worker had to climb in and sweep the last of the contents and any dirt out. Not a very nice job, I would think!

In the barn, was a mealie loft where mealies on the cob were stored and very hot, it was too, under a low thin roof. Behind the barn was the large cattle byre and then the long milking shed with a room at the end where the chaff was cut.

Chapter 18

Dual Control
Written By Donald McLeod

This article was entered in "Car" magazine's "Motoring Memories" competition and was published

During the early part of the 1920's, my father kept our farming family in transport with his Model-T Ford. At the time, the family consisted of Grandpa, Grandma, my mother and father, an uncle and aunt, and myself. I was still a child. However, when my father went to work a farm some distance away, the family was left without any means of getting from A to B, all the riding horses having been sold off to make way for dairy cows.

About this time, I left the farm with my parents but when I returned (after my father's untimely death), I was met by an amazing sight. Grandma had bought a motor car! Grandpa had no idea about driving whatsoever. He had a slight mechanical knowledge when it came to the farm machinery, but how to drive a motor vehicle?...... Never! The answer was to train my uncle and aunt how to drive. My uncle was a mechanical genius but there was just one drawback - he was completely blind!

This was the procedure. My aunt, a little woman, was propped up on cushions behind the wheel of the car (a slightly newer version Model-T than my father's). My uncle made sure that the parking brake was properly applied (on a Model-T, this put the epicyclical transmission into neutral) and would go round to the front of the car to crank-start it.

With the old Tin Lizzie shaking like a jelly, he would climb into the passenger's seat, assume a crouching position, leaning to the right, being careful not to get into the driver's line of sight and adjust the hand throttle on the steering wheel, as well as the ignition advance, before giving my aunt the go-ahead.

Entire journeys were made in this way. All my aunt did was to steer and apply the brakes; while my uncle controlled the speed, adjusted the advance, and told her when to change gears. It was in every way "dual" control. And amazing but true, this combination actually had a driving licence! What's more, I never heard of them ever having been involved in an accident, or the car giving any trouble. This latter was unusual at a time as cars were not as reliable as they are today. Mind you, traffic was sparse, and I suppose the locals gave them a wide berth when they saw them coming. And, of course, a round trip would not exceed twenty-five kilometres.

This state of affairs lasted until my uncle decided to move to the South Coast, so dear old Grandma had to sell her Model-T, leaving the family without wheeled transport, until I obtained a driving licence many years later.

Cars in the late 1920's and 1930's

My life interest has been the motor car. As long as I can remember, I have been intrigued by cars and I am still interested to see all the latest models on our roads.

Despite the fact that the cars of yesterday looked so very different to their modern counterparts, there is basically very little difference - an internal combustion engine, driving through a plate clutch, a transmission, to a final drive. At that time nearly always rear wheel drive (while today the front wheels are usually the driven wheels) but there are exceptions today as there were exceptions in the days of which I write.

One thing is certain; there were no cars from the Far East back then. All the cars on our roads were American, the favoured country of origin, or British: Cars of that time were built more like the three-ton trucks of today, with a robust box section chassis and heavy sheet-metal work.

Among the names that I can remember that went off the market before WW2, were Bean, Jowet, Erskin, Sussex, Reo, Trojan, Orbin, Essex, Graham and Graham-Page, Willis Knight (Willis of the famous wartime Jeep) Crosley, Maxwell, (the forerunner of Chrysler) La Sall, Singer, Sunbeam. Some of the stalwarts only ceased production after WW2. Packard, Hudson, Studebaker, De Soto, Riley, Wolsey, Morris, Austin, Vauxhall, Hillman, Triumph.

Petrol Bowsers were few and far between, and most farmers bought their petrol in four-gallon tins; the ubiquitous petrol-paraffin tin was at that time as popular as the modern plastic shopping bag. The tin made of heavy sheet-tin could be cut open at the top and a stout wire handle attached and used for a multitude of purposes, carrying water, potatoes, mealies, measuring anything and everything! Sad was the day that it went out of production.

The wheels of the cars were not at all like the wheels of today. There were wooden spokes on the very early cars that I can remember, and then came the wire spokes like a bicycle wheel and then the pressed steel disc took over. Most cars in my early days were "tourers" - soft top cars - and then the hard top became popular.

The model T Ford (the farmer's car) stopped production in 1928 to be followed by the model A. In 1932, Henry Ford brought out the Ford V8 - a very advanced car for that time with a light body and big engine, which revolutionized the motor world, soon to be followed by the Essex Terraplane. From then on the modern concept of the powerful engine and speed, was started. A Willis 77, a light car for the time, cost under two hundred pounds in 1936 and petrol was 1/6 a gallon when I started motoring in 1940!!

The one thing that was very crude was the suspension system - leaf springs all round with very crude shock-absorbers.

A rough ride but such fun to see the advances over the years.

Section 3

Chapter 19

The Lloyds

Written By Gwynyth Lloyd Johnson, Sister Of Felicity Lloyd

Sadly we didn't ever meet our Grandmother Catherine Lloyd, although she lived until the 1930s, and we hardly knew our Lloyd relatives at all. Grandfather John Andrew Lloyd had died in about 1906 when our father, Frank was eleven.

Frank Lloyd was born in East London and sometime after John Andrew had died, the family moved to the Germiston/Johannesburg area. Frank lived with the family and worked there until sometime after the General Strike of 1922 when he moved down to Natal, and pretty much lost touch with his family. We had a couple of brief visits from one of his brothers, Gordon, and his wife, and his sister Lily Blackbeard found us in Bellair in about 1954, and we enjoyed several very pleasant visits from her family. But those were the only contacts we ever had with the huge Lloyd family.

Our Lloyd ancestors include three different 1820 Settler families all of whose paths would cross again and intertwine. The Lloyds, the Kidsons and the Piries. All these families came from London. The fourth family making up the set of my father's grandparents, were the

Doyles, who were earlier Cape Settlers, and had come from Ireland, France, Holland and the North Western part of Germany around Cologne that was known as North Rhine Westphalia.

Henry James and Rebecca Lloyd were part of Baillies party of 1820 Settlers who settled in Cuylerville, near the mouth of the Great Fish River, north of Port Alfred.

William and Anna Kidson and Robert and Mary Ann Pirie were in Willsons party and they settled in the Bathurst area about 20 km south west of Cuylerville. I wonder, did the settlers know that they were going to be the human buffer between the expanding British colony in the Cape which was pushing ever northwards and eastwards and the Xhosa people who were living in the eastern Cape at the time?

The settlers certainly had a tough life, but once there, they had little option but to get on as best they could, fighting off intruders and learning to farm land in an unfamiliar climate.

The Lloyds and Piries hadn't been farmers in England, having come from London. Robert Pirie was a baker and Henry Lloyd was a worsted Weaver. William Kidson was an English farmer, born in Staindrop, County Durham, who had moved south to Essex where he had married Anna Maria Parke in Saffron Walden.

The settlers landed in Algoa Bay in 1820, the Lloyds having sailed on the ship *Chapman* and the Piries and Kidsons on *La Belle Alliance*. A bleak windswept landscape awaited them. Mile after mile of sand dunes backed by scrubby bush. Three houses and one reed thatched hut was all the settlement consisted of. Soldiers had erected rows and rows of tents on the beach to accommodate the arriving settlers.

A frightening incident happened in the first few days which almost had tragic consequences. Charles Lloyd, the youngest child and just a toddler, had wandered from the tent off into the bush and was lost. A search party was mounted and the bush searched. Movement was heard at one point and the searchers called out, but there was no reply, so they guessed it might have been a wild animal. A soldier cocked his gun, ready to fire, but just then little Charles wandered out of the bush, unharmed, much to everyone's relief.

After a week in their tent, Henry James and Rebecca Lloyd with their three small children set off by ox wagon on a 10 day trek through the bush and along rough tracks heading north east up the coast.

Henry James Lloyd *Rebecca (Poulton) Lloyd*
1791 – 1863 *1792 - 1874*

Along the way they passed the Theopolis Mission where yet another player in our ancestral story would be living. Thomas Doyle and his wife Catharina de Waal moved there from Cape Town in the 1820s and their son William Shepherd Doyle was born there in about 1831.

The Settler parties crossed over the sandbanks at the mouth of the Kowie River at present day Port Alfred. Willsons Party turned inland to settle in the Bathurst area, and Baillies Party continued north for another 20 km where they crossed the mouth of the East and West Kleinemond rivers and settled on the area between the Kleinemond and Great Fish Rivers, which, at that stage, was the north eastern border of the Cape Colony. The

Settler Party named the area Cuylerville in honour of the Landdrost of Uitenhage, Colonel Cuyler, who had accompanied the party to show them the way, and had shown great kindness to the settlers.

Early hardships saw their first primitive houses and crops swept away by floodwaters but they faced these adversities manfully, and started again, choosing more suitable sites for their houses and cultivation, above and away from the streams that had flooded.

Fortunately, the Lloyds were healthy, and their family grew to eleven with the birth of eight more children in South Africa. They had seven sons before their first daughter was born.

Children had to accept huge responsibilities at a young age. Our ancestor, Great Grandfather John, was the first Lloyd to be born in South Africa. When the birth was imminent in 1821, Henry, Rebecca and two-year-old Charles went to Grahamstown, leaving the two older boys, Henry Thomas and William, aged 7 and 5, on their own, without knowing how long they would be away. Before they left Henry James killed and cured a goat and hung it in a tree instructing the boys to take care of it and not to eat too much at a time. They had neighbours on nearby farms but the two little boys managed to look after themselves, and ate very little of the goat which was still hanging in the tree and was smelling rather bad by the time Henry and Rebecca returned with Charles and baby John.

The settler families were each granted 100 acres of land if they remained on it for three years. Henry James Lloyd named his farm Red Mount, but found the size inadequate and as time went on and a couple of other families left the area he took up the neighbouring farm, Bellevue. These farms can be seen on Google Earth between the Kap River Conservancy and Cuylerville Church. The red soil is visible on Google, and the area remains farmland and appears relatively undeveloped.

After early disastrous attempts to grow crops, including having them burned by the Xhosas, Henry James changed to cattle farming where he had much more success and he built up a sizeable herd. In 1846 one hundred and eighty of his cattle were driven off by Xhosa raiders. A few months later some of the cattle were recaptured and he got seventy two head of cattle back.

The settlers built a church at Cuylerville which still exists, along with the Settlers Cemetery. Three Lloyd sons, James, Edmund and George are buried there.

A stone Kraal was added to the church which acted as a fort during the many attacks from the Xhosas, and which prevented assegais being thrown into the church. During the Frontier War of 1846 to 1847 it was defended heroically by the local settlers. A Lychgate was later erected in the cemetery and it has two pink marble memorial tablets commemorating the defence of Cuylerville in 1846. The first tablet lists 16 men who bravely defended the settlement. John and Robert Lloyd are among the sixteen names. The second tablet commemorates the names of other men who are known to have taken full part in the defence, including Henry and William Lloyd. Inside the lager were five unfit men, fifteen women and twenty one children.

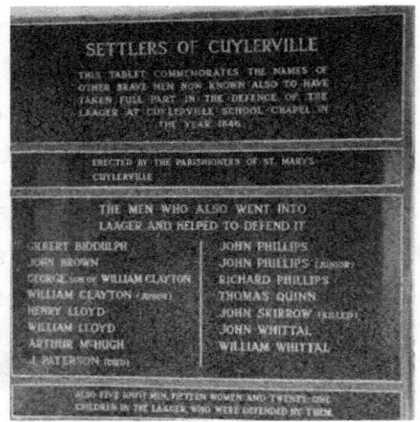

1820 Settler Memorial Plaques inside Lychgate

Photos of Cuylerville Church and Lychgate kindly supplied by Sarah Elkington Auberge

Amongst the names on the list is Gilbert Biddulph. Simon Burnet Biddulph's family were also part of Baillies Party. Some of the family eventually moved up to the Orange Free State and their great granddaughter Alice married Ted McLeod from Byrne, and were ancestors of Magnus MacLeod.

The Lloyds defended Cuylerville many times over the twenty seven years they lived there. Their crops were burnt and cattle stolen, and they were attacked with assegais, but they loved the place and were very attached to it. However, it was a rather remote area and after the 1846 war, some of the sons started travelling north of the Fish River to Kaffraria to trade with the black people in the area. In 1847 Red Mount was put up for sale and then

Henry James and most of his children's families left the area and went further inland to Fort Beaufort, where he continued farming and trading, with family nearby. Henry James and Rebecca lived in Fort Beaufort for the rest of their lives, and many of the grandchildren were baptised there, and when Rebecca died in 1874, some years after Henry, it is recorded that she left one hundred and ten descendants, so the Lloyds had really thrived.

John Lloyd and Mary Ann nee Pirie

John Lloyd did not follow his parents and the rest of the family to Fort Beaufort but went farming in the Albany area. He had married Mary Ann Pirie in Cuylerville in 1844. The Piries had lived about twenty km away in Bathurst which is between Port Alfred and Grahamstown. John and Mary Ann moved around the Eastern Cape farming in different areas, initially in the Albany district where in 1850, their son John Andrew Lloyd, our grandfather, was born, and later he was farming near the Great Fish River Mouth, and by 1867 he was living on a farm called Ferndale, five miles from East London. Not much is known about John unfortunately, but a niece of his, Millicent Lloyd, once met him in Queenstown and said he was a happy person, always full of fun. John was buried in the West Bank Cemetery, East London in 1897.

In the meantime, the Doyle's had moved from Theopolis Mission where their son, William Shepherd Doyle had been born in 1831, to live on a farm "Longridge" in Peddie. Thomas Doyle had come to South Africa from Wexford, Ireland, in 1806. He was in the 21st Light Dragoons division of the British Army which had come to Cape Town to fight the Dutch for control of the Cape, to prevent the Refreshment Station and control of the sea route to the East Indies, from falling into Napoleon's hands. Thomas was the Military Chaplain at the Cape, and he married Catharina Elizabeth de Waal in Cape Town in 1816 and was discharged from the army on 3 June 1817. They moved to the Theopolis Mission in the Eastern Cape where he was a teacher and Lay Missionary. More about Catharina later as she was herself a 6th generation South African, with a very interesting genealogy.

William Kidson and his wife Anna continued to live in Bathurst, and their daughter Elizabeth Kidson was born in 1829. Elizabeth Kidson married William Shepherd Doyle in 1855 and their daughter, Catharina de Waal Doyle, our grandmother, known as Catharine, was born in King Williamstown in 1859.

Elizabeth Kidson and William Shepherd Doyle Parents of our grandmother Catherine de Waal Doyle

The Kidsons were a seemingly well-to-do family and the 1820 Settler website informs us that William and Anna were buried in a vault in the cemetery on the old Hartley Homestead property in Bathurst. When the grave was renovated and restored in about 1912, the vault was discovered underneath with William's lead sealed coffin and the remains of Anna, embalmed and perfectly preserved with unmarked skin and masses of red hair around her head. Perhaps that is where our father and two of his sisters inherited their red hair from.

Anna Maria (Parke) Kidson

John Andrew Lloyd's movements are not known, but presumably he went, as a boy, with his parents John and Mary Ann Lloyd, to East London where they were living in 1867 when their youngest daughter Amy Rachel was born. John Andrew became a Transport Rider, travelling inland to the Diamond Fields. When he was thirty, in 1880, he married Catharina de Waal Doyle in the Peddie Methodist Church. They lived in the East London suburb of Southernwood with their family of nine children, including their son Tilney Franks "Ginger" Lloyd who was born in 1895. Sadly, on one of his trips inland, John Andrew contracted a fever and met an untimely death in about 1906 leaving Catharine and their young family in financial hardship.

Frank Lloyd 1949

Source "The Family of Henry James and Rebecca Lloyd" written by Margaret Lloyd, Grahamstown 1984

The Ancestry of Catharina Elizabeth de Waal 1790 - 1863

Catharina's ancestry was partly French Huguenot and the rest a mixture of Dutch and German.

The Huguenots had escaped from France to Holland after the revocation of the Edict of Nantes in 1685 when it became illegal to be a Protestant in France. Although they had been prohibited from leaving France, about 400,000 Huguenots eventually managed to escape to various countries, taking their Calvinist faith with them. Our ancestors went to Amsterdam.

The French families had a good working knowledge of the wine industry in Normandy and Flanders, and were offered the opportunity of joining the Dutch East India Company Settlement in the Cape and becoming wine farmers, supplying the local population and the passing ships. They arrived in South Africa before 1700. The Huguenots had quite a big influence on the young Cape Colony and also on the emerging Afrikaans language, which was a simpler version of High Dutch. The first five Prime Ministers of South Africa were of Huguenot descent.

Catharina's Huguenot ancestor families were le Roux, Neel, de la Batte and le Lievre. The le Lievres changed their name to the Dutch version, de Haas, which also means The Hare. And Guillaume Neel also in due course, once in South Africa, changed his name to Willem Nel.

The le Roux name remained unchanged, and JC le Roux is still the brand name of one of the big wineries.

Jean le Roux from Normandie was initially allocated a farm Het Vlackeland, in Daljosaphat north of Paarl. And some years later he was allocated Langverwacht in Stellenbosch. He married Marie de Haas from Lille, Flanders.

Guillaume Neel from Rouen in Normandie was first allocated farm Bootmans Drift in Drakenstein, and later Blaauklippen in Stellenbosch. He married Jeanne de la Batte from Saumur, Anjou.

Guillaume de Haas from Flanders settled in Stellenbosch, and later in Daljosaphat, and his daughter Marie de Haas married Jean le Roux.

Catharina's de Waal surname came from her Great Grandfather, Johannes de Waal who arrived on board the ship *Doornik* from Amsterdam in 1715. Johannes worked for the Dutch East India Company (DEIC) as Quartermaster at the Cape Town Castle, and later as Sexton at the Cape Church. He was a wealthy man and owned many properties. Wale St in Cape Town, and de Waal Drive are named after him.

Catharina's other Dutch and German ancestors came to the Cape as employees of the DEIC, or Free Settlers and farmers.

Jan Mostert was a farmer and farmed east of Tierberg.

Cornelius Uys was a sailor.

Jacob Cloete was a Corporal in the service of the DEIC, a Free Burgher and a farmer. He arrived in 1655.

Juriaan Franz Appel worked for the DEIC.

Cornelis van Eck worked for DEIC.

Source: The Huguenots of South Africa 1688-1988 written by Pieter Coertzen

Authors Note (Gwynyth Lloyd)

My father had always told us that his mother was Catherine de Waal and that they were Huguenots, however there was no trace of her on any of the avenues of research that I followed, and I ascertained that de Waal wasn't a Huguenot name. I was intrigued by this and my mission became to find who all my ancestors were, and what had brought them to South Africa. Then followed years of brick walls in my research, until a "Eureka Day" happened in about 2014 and I discovered a transcribed Church Record from Peddie Methodist Church, recording the marriage of John Andrew Lloyd and Catherine de Waal Doyle in 1880 in Peddie in the Cape. I remembered that my father had said he played with his Doyle cousins as a boy in East London and from then onwards everything fell into place. de Waal was Catherine's second name, not her surname, and with the help of Prof le Roux from Cape Town, and other contributors to Wikitree, I had the joy of discovering our Huguenot and early Cape ancestry.

Chapter 20

Our Immigrant Ancestors

Felicity, Michael and Gwynyth Lloyd have twenty eight Immigrant Ancestors, all from the UK and North Western Europe.

English Ancestors: Arrival in SA

1. Henry James LLOYD   1820
2. Rebecca POULTON   1820
3. Robert PIRIE   1820
4. Mary Rachel HORNE   1820
5. William KIDSON   1820
6. Anna Maria PARKE   1820
7. George More MCLEOD   1850
8. Ellen CRISTALL   1850
9. Mary Ann COLE   1861

Irish Ancestors:

1. Thomas DOYLE   1805

Dutch Ancestors:

1. Cornelis VAN ECK   abt 1700
2. Johannes DE WAAL   1715

3. Jan MOSTERT abt 1688
4. Elizabeth NIEMEYER abt 1688
5. Catharina HARMANS bef 1689
6. Cornelis UIJS bef 1704
7. Dirkje MATTYSEN bef 1704
8. Juriann Franz APPEL bef 1658
9. Jannetjie FERNANDUS bef 1658

German Ancestors:

1. Elizabeth SCHMIDT abt 1700
2. Jacob CLOETE 1655
3. Sophia RADERGOERTGENS 1655
4. John Frederick BAUMANN 1851

French Ancestors:

1. Jean LE ROUX abt 1691
2. Guillaume DE HAAS abt 1700
3. Marie-Catherine DURIER abt 1700
4. Guillaume NEEL 1688
5. Jeanne DE LA BATTE 1688

I have divided this information into 4 sections, one for each of my Father's and Mother's families, listing just the immigrants to South Africa

1. Vera Edna McLeod's Paternal Ancestors – McLeod and CRISTALL
2. Vera Edna McLeod's Maternal Ancestors – BAUMANN and COLE
3. Tilney Frank Lloyd's Paternal Ancestors – LLOYD, POULTON, PIRIE and HORNE
4. Tilney Frank Lloyd's Maternal Ancestors – DOYLE. De WAAL, KIDSON and PARKE.

McLeod

- George More MC LEOD 1814 – 1881 Born Kirk Levington, Yorkshire and his wife…
- Ellen CRISTALL 1813 – 1888 Born in London

George and Ellen emigrated to Natal in 1850 with the Byrne Settlers on board the ship *Minerva* which was wrecked off Durban. They were granted farmland in the Byrne Valley near Richmond in Natal

Baumann

- John Frederick BAUMANN 1824 – 1897 Born in Niederstetten, Germany

John settled in Durban in 1851 and opened a Bakers Shop in West Street later the same year

He married Mary Anne COLE in Durban in 1864

- Mary Ann COLE 1842 – 1909 Born in Leytonstone, Essex, England

Mary Ann went to South Africa in about 1861 with her aunt and uncle, James Lambert, who had won the contract to harden the Point Road from the Durban Docks to the town. The job proved more costly than estimated, and James went bankrupt, returning to England in 1864, leaving Mary Ann in Durban where she married John BAUMANN. She returned to England in 1867 for the birth of her daughter Florence whom she left with her parents in Leytonstone, whilst she worked as a Stewardess on ships sailing from England to many parts of the world including Australia, South Africa, Hong Kong and Singapore. She lived in Hong Kong for about four years, marrying an Englishman who was living there, then returned to England early in 1879. Some years later she returned to Durban, and after John Baumann had died in 1897, she married a Mr Marsh who had been involved in building the Connaught Bridge over the Umgeni River in Durban. When Mr Marsh died, she lived with her daughter's McLeod family in Malvern.

Lloyd

- Henry James LLOYD 1791 – 1863 born in London and his wife…

- Rebecca POULTON 1792 – 1874 born in Hampstead Heath, London

  Henry and Rebecca were 1820 Settlers in BAILLIES Party who arrived in Algoa Bay on the ship *Chapman*. They lived in the Cuylerville and Fort Beaufort areas of the Eastern Cape

- Robert PIRIE 1785 – 1827 born in England and his wife...

- Mary Rachel HORNE 1796 – abt 1836 born in England.

  Robert and Mary were 1820 Settlers in WILLSONS Party who arrived in Algoa Bay on the ship *La Belle Alliance* Their daughter Mary Ann PIRIE married John LLOYD, son of Henry James and Rebecca LLOYD

Doyle

- William KIDSON 1784 – 1869 Born in Staindrop, County Durham, England and his wife...

- Anna Maria PARKE 1788 – 1843 Born in Saffron Waldon, Essex, England

William and his wife Anna Maria were 1820 Settlers in WILLSONS Party who arrived in Algoa Bay on the ship *La Belle Alliance*. They settled in the Bathurst area then East London, and had a daughter, Elizabeth who married William DOYLE.

- Thomas DOYLE 1778 – 1851 Born in Ireland and died in Grahamstown. Thomas arrived in Cape Town in 1805/1806 as a soldier in the 21st Light Dragoons fighting for the British against the Dutch for control of the Cape Colony. After discharge from the army in 1817 Thomas DOYLE married Catharina de Waal.
- Catharina Elizabeth DE WAAL was born in 1790 in Stellenbosch and they moved to the Grahamstown district where Thomas became a teacher and Lay Preacher in the Theopolis Mission. Their son William DOYLE married Elizabeth KIDSON, daughter of 1820 Settlers William and Anna Maria KIDSON. Catharina De WAAL was herself, a 6th generation South African and she had seventeen immigrant ancestors, nine from Holland, three from Germany and five from France, listed below:

1. Cornelis VAN ECK 1663 – 1721 Born in De Pumer, Netherlands and his wife…

2. Elizabeth SCHMIDT 1663 – aft 1721 Born in Ratingen, Dusseldorf, North Rhine Westphalia

   Cornelis and Elizabeth arrived in Cape Town abt 1700

   Their daughter Elizabeth VAN ECK married Johannes DE WAAL

3. Johannes DE WAAL 1692 – 1768 Born in Amsterdam, Netherlands. Died in Cape Town.

Johannes arrived in Cape Town on the ship *Doornik* in 1715 worked for the Dutch East India Company as Quartermaster and owned many properties in Cape Town including Jan de Waal House in Bree St and the house in Waal St where the Maleier Museum is. Wale/Waal St is named after him. He married Elizabeth VAN ECK in Cape Town.

4. Jan MOSTERT 1646 – 1729 Born in Utrecht, Netherlands and his wife…

5. Elizabeth NIEMEYER 1670 – 1720 Born in Deventer, Overijssel, Netherlands

    Jan and Elizabeth arrived in Cape Town before 1688 and farmed east of Tierberg.

6. Jacob CLOETE abt 1630 – 1693 Born in Kurfurstentum, Cologne, North Rhine Westphalia and wife…

7. Sophia RADERGOERTGENS 1624 – 1665 Born in Cologne, North Rhine Westphalia

Jacob and Sophia are believed to have arrived at Cape Town in 1655. He was a Corporal in the service of the Dutch East India Company, a Free Burgher and a farmer.

Their son Gerrit CLOETE married Catharina HARMANS

8. Catharina HARMANS 1656 – 1698 Born in Middleburg, Zeeland, Netherlands. Died in Stellenbosch. She married Gerrit Cloete the son of Jacob CLOETE and Sophia RADERGOERTGENS

9. Cornelis UYS 1671 – 1714 Born in Amsterdam, Netherlands and his wife…

10. Dirkje MATTHYSEN 1673 - 1714 Born in Leiden, South Holland

Cornelis was a sailor. He and Dirkje arrived in the Cape before 1704

11. Guillaume DE HAAS 1658 - 1713 Born in Lille, Flanders, France and his wife….

12. Marie-Catherine DURIER 1660 – 1725 Born in Lille, Flanders, France

Guillaume and Marie were Huguenot Protestants fleeing religious intolerance in France.

They and their daughter Marie DE HAAS arrived in Cape Town in about 1700 and settled in Stellenbosch then later in Daljosaphat, Paarl. Marie DE HAAS married Jean LE ROUX.

13. Jean LE ROUX 1676 – 1752 Born in Normandy, France

He was a Huguenot Protestant and arrived in Cape Town about 1691 and was allocated a farm Vlakkeland in Paarl in 1692, then in 1712 was allocated farm Langverwacht in Stellenbosch. He married Marie DE HAAS. The JC Le Roux Winery is still located in Stellenbosch on the original Devon Valley Farm.

14. Guillaume NEEL 1663 – 1738 Born in Rouen, France and his wife …

15. Jeanne DE LA BATTE 1666 – 1734   Born in Saumur, Anjou, France

Guillaume and Jeanne were Huguenot Protestants fleeing religious intolerance in France.

They arrived in Cape Town in 1688 and were granted farm Blaauklip in Stellenbosch in 1690.

Their name NEEL changed to NEL. Blaauklippen Winery is still on the same Stellenbosch farm.

16. Juriaan Franz APPEL 1638 – 1672 Born in Brederwiede, Overijssel, Netherlands and his wife…

17. Jannetjie FERNANDUS 1640 - Born in Courtrai, Flanders

Juriaan and Jannetjie arrived in Cape Town in 1658. Juriaan worked in the service of the DEIC.

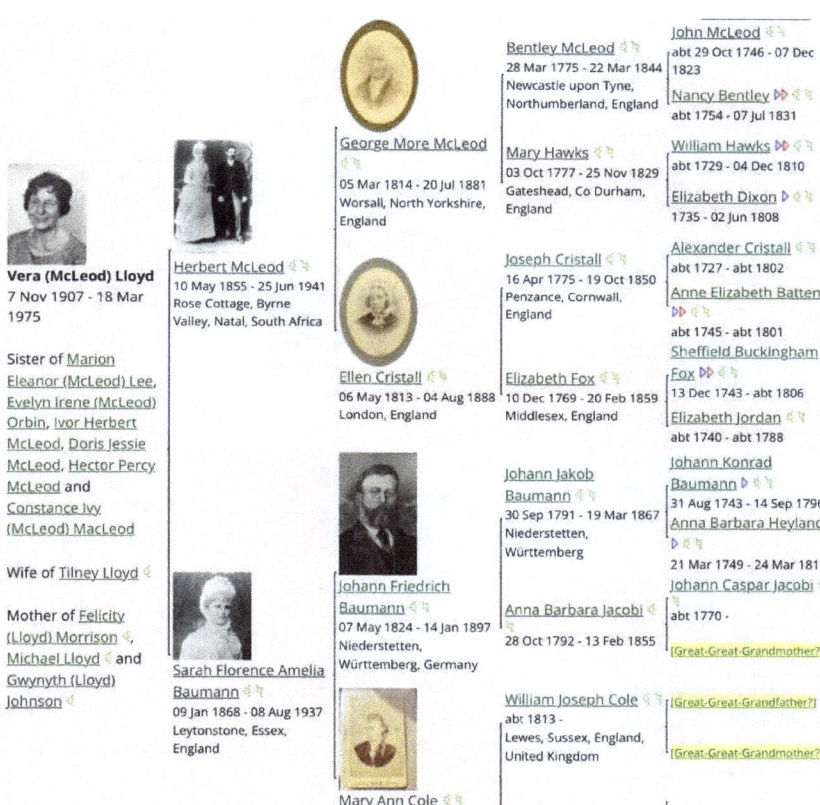

Ancestral Family Tree of Vera (McLeod) Lloyd from Wikitree

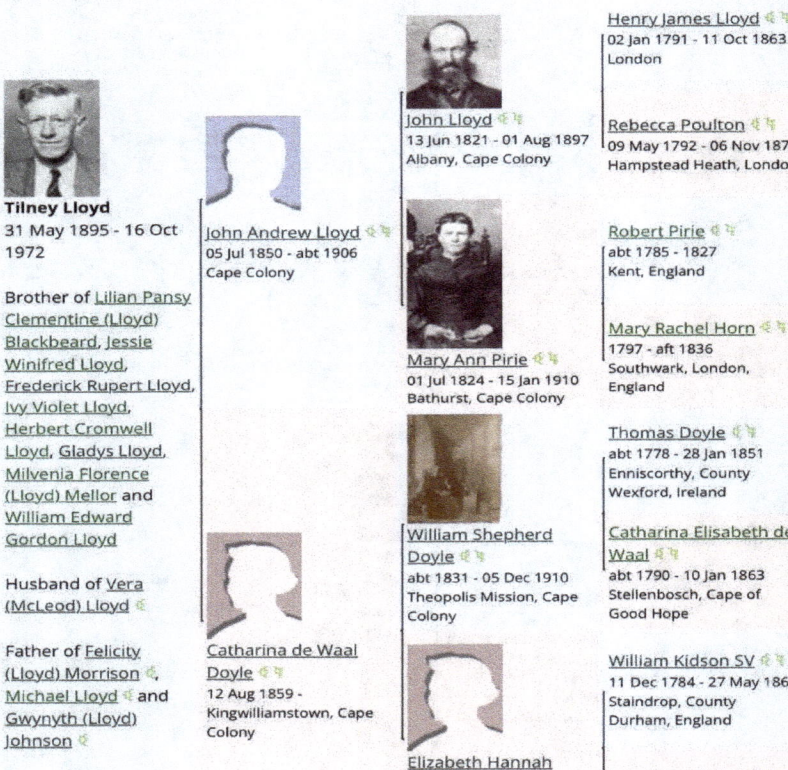

Tilney Lloyd
31 May 1895 - 16 Oct 1972

Brother of Lilian Pansy Clementine (Lloyd) Blackbeard, Jessie Winifred Lloyd, Frederick Rupert Lloyd, Ivy Violet Lloyd, Herbert Cromwell Lloyd, Gladys Lloyd, Milvenia Florence (Lloyd) Mellor and William Edward Gordon Lloyd

Husband of Vera (McLeod) Lloyd

Father of Felicity (Lloyd) Morrison, Michael Lloyd and Gwynyth (Lloyd) Johnson

John Andrew Lloyd
05 Jul 1850 - abt 1906
Cape Colony

Catharina de Waal Doyle
12 Aug 1859 -
Kingwilliamstown, Cape Colony

John Lloyd
13 Jun 1821 - 01 Aug 1897
Albany, Cape Colony

Mary Ann Pirie
01 Jul 1824 - 15 Jan 1910
Bathurst, Cape Colony

William Shepherd Doyle
abt 1831 - 05 Dec 1910
Theopolis Mission, Cape Colony

Elizabeth Hannah Kidson
06 Feb 1829 - abt 1905
Bathurst, Cape Colony, South Africa

Henry James Lloyd
02 Jan 1791 - 11 Oct 1863
London

Rebecca Poulton
09 May 1792 - 06 Nov 1874
Hampstead Heath, London

Robert Pirie
abt 1785 - 1827
Kent, England

Mary Rachel Horn
1797 - aft 1836
Southwark, London, England

Thomas Doyle
abt 1778 - 28 Jan 1851
Enniscorthy, County Wexford, Ireland

Catharina Elisabeth de Waal
abt 1790 - 10 Jan 1863
Stellenbosch, Cape of Good Hope

William Kidson SV
11 Dec 1784 - 27 May 1869
Staindrop, County Durham, England

Anna Maria Parke
18 Apr 1788 - 18 May 1843
Saffron Walden, Essex, England

Ancestral Family Tree of Tilney Franks Lloyd from Wikitree

Fun fact. Our distant connection to British Royal Family via my father's great grandmother Anna Maria Parke.

Ancestral Family Tree of Catharina Elizabeth de Waal from Wikitree

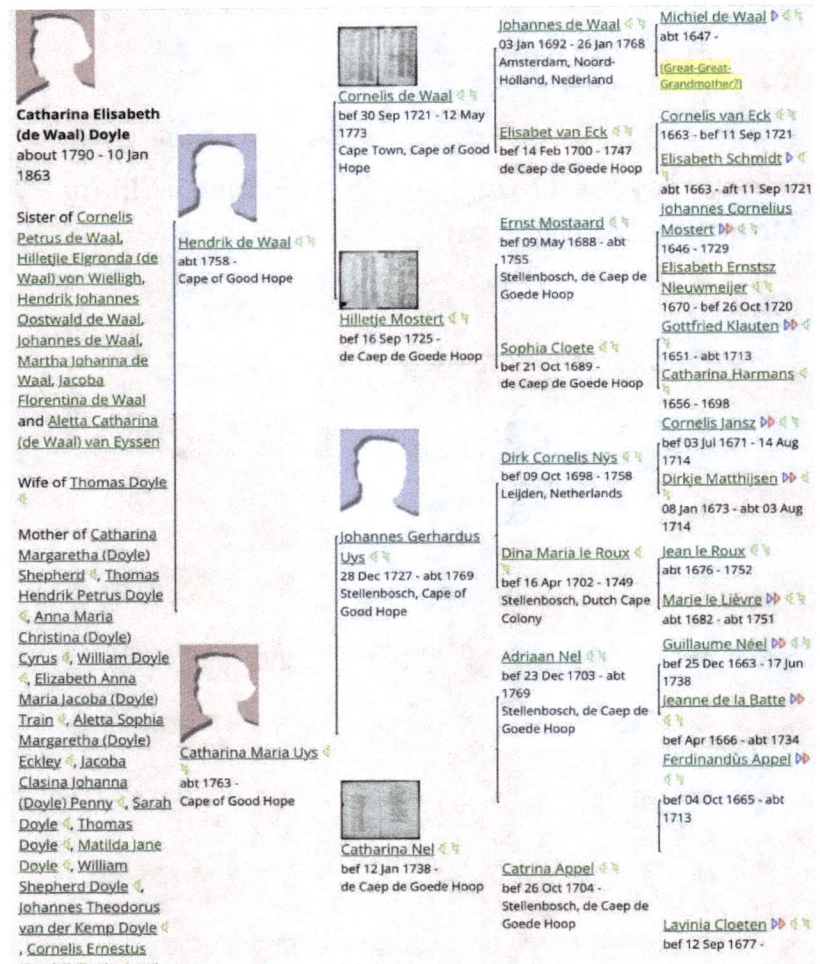

Catharina Elisabeth (de Waal) Doyle
about 1790 - 10 Jan 1863

Sister of Cornelis Petrus de Waal, Hilletjie Elgronda (de Waal) von Wielligh, Hendrik Johannes Oostwald de Waal, Johannes de Waal, Martha Johanna de Waal, Jacoba Florentina de Waal and Aletta Catharina (de Waal) van Eyssen

Wife of Thomas Doyle

Mother of Catharina Margaretha (Doyle) Shepherd, Thomas Hendrik Petrus Doyle, Anna Maria Christina (Doyle) Cyrus, William Doyle, Elizabeth Anna Maria Jacoba (Doyle) Train, Aletta Sophia Margaretha (Doyle) Eckley, Jacoba Clasina Johanna (Doyle) Penny, Sarah Doyle, Thomas Doyle, Matilda Jane Doyle, William Shepherd Doyle, Johannes Theodorus van der Kemp Doyle, Cornelis Ernestus Hendrik Doyle and

Hendrik de Waal
abt 1758 -
Cape of Good Hope

Hilletje Mostert
bef 16 Sep 1725 -
de Caep de Goede Hoop

Johannes Gerhardus Uys
28 Dec 1727 - abt 1769
Stellenbosch, Cape of Good Hope

Catharina Maria Uys
abt 1763 -
Cape of Good Hope

Catharina Nel
bef 12 Jan 1738 -
de Caep de Goede Hoop

Cornelis de Waal
bef 30 Sep 1721 - 12 May 1773
Cape Town, Cape of Good Hope

Johannes de Waal
03 Jan 1692 - 26 Jan 1768
Amsterdam, Noord-Holland, Nederland

Elisabet van Eck
bef 14 Feb 1700 - 1747
de Caep de Goede Hoop

Ernst Mostaard
bef 09 May 1688 - abt 1755
Stellenbosch, de Caep de Goede Hoop

Sophia Cloete
bef 21 Oct 1689 -
de Caep de Goede Hoop

Dirk Cornelis Nys
bef 09 Oct 1698 - 1758
Leijden, Netherlands

Dina Maria le Roux
bef 16 Apr 1702 - 1749
Stellenbosch, Dutch Cape Colony

Adriaan Nel
bef 23 Dec 1703 - abt 1769
Stellenbosch, de Caep de Goede Hoop

Catrina Appel
bef 26 Oct 1704 -
Stellenbosch, de Caep de Goede Hoop

Michiel de Waal
abt 1647 -
[Great-Great-Grandmother?]

Cornelis van Eck
1663 - bef 11 Sep 1721

Elisabeth Schmidt
abt 1663 - aft 11 Sep 1721

Johannes Cornelius Mostert
1646 - 1729

Elisabeth Ernstsz Nieuwmeijer
1670 - bef 26 Oct 1720

Gottfried Klauten
1651 - abt 1713

Catharina Harmans
1656 - 1698

Cornelis Jansz
bef 03 Jul 1671 - 14 Aug 1714

Dirkje Matthijsen
08 Jan 1673 - abt 03 Aug 1714

Jean le Roux
abt 1676 - 1752

Marie le Lièvre
abt 1682 - abt 1751

Guillaume Néel
bef 25 Dec 1663 - 17 Jun 1738

Jeanne de la Batte
bef Apr 1666 - abt 1734

Ferdinandus Appel
bef 04 Oct 1665 - abt 1713

Lavinia Cloeten
bef 12 Sep 1677 -

Appendices

1. Researchers

We are grateful to the members of the family who have taken trouble and time to try to uncover the history of our branch of the MacLeod clan.

Llewellyn Wynn McLeod b 1847 in England who inspired his children to take an interest. Corresponded with South African George More and Edward McLeod.

Roderick MacLeod b 1877 son of the above, who with his brother Donald b 1885 did much investigating, writing letters etc. pre-WWI and put together an invaluable Family Tree book and gave it to siblings.

Evelyn MacLeod sister of the above who went to Edinburgh and copied out many records hoping to confirm possible Dysart birthplace with no success. Pre WWI.

Angus MacLeod nephew of the above who made many enquiries in the 1970s and who discovered the DOB of John b 1746 in Newcastle.

Magnus and Byrne McLeod, descended from the S African branch who made further discoveries.

Hugh McLeod, son of Magnus and Byrne.

Gwynyth Johnson in Australia also from South Africa who consolidated what she discovered and put details on Wikitree ensuring a correct record.

Herbert McLeod (Herbie) who instilled in his children an awareness and interest in their McLeod heritage

2. **Interesting snippets from Herbert McLeod's "Where is it" notebook 1917 – 1939**

Herbert's notebook was an A-Z "Where is it" book. Entries were categorized and recorded alphabetically, for example A: Aeroplane, B: Bessie, boots, braces, F: Florence, Frank, father's old clock, free railway passes, L: Lifebuoy soap, lovely kiss.

NOTE: Unless otherwise state, all entries are from the notebook. *Italics* are a direct quote from the source. Birdie was his nickname for his wife Florence.

19 November 1917	*23 years since coming from Byrne*
22 October 1917	*Moved to 18 room Railway Offices. Not long there*
13 December 1917	*Birdie gone to Dbn to manage a business Evelyn has bought*
23 April 1918	*Moved all of us on 23.4.18 from Malvern to 435 Point Road Durban*
25 June 1918	*Doctor Murray Gray is the RMO for this district 435 Point Road and his telephone number is 738, his address is number 51 Manning Road*
31 July 1918	*Heard that Bessie is very bad now not likely to survive*
31 July 1918	*Evelyn gone to work at Nils Rust Creamery Left sometime in January 1919*

5 August 1918	*Bessie passed away*
24 August 1918	*"Our Day" was off duty at 1pm for the afternoon*
8 September 1918	*We all went to Isipingo Beach*
14 February 1919	*Birdie and Evelyn sold business in 435*
1 April 1919	*Moved all of us on 1.4.19 from 435 to 556 Point Road*
13 May 1919	*As Birdie has a shop now and do not know how much it costs her, have decided not to book more (Author's note: he was referring to train tickets)*
1 July 1919	*Shoulder injured by fall on Beach, could not go on duty*
6 August 1919	*Resumed duty after fall. Sick fund £7.3 deducted as from October 1919*
18 September 1919	*Evelyn married to Mr Orbin*
1 October 1919	*War Bonus altered, increased substantially, past put onto Salary & what is called War Bonus is £44 P.A*
1 January 1920	*War Bonus increased to £72 per annum*
Later entries in this regard ...	*War Bonus increased from £72 to £93 from 1.4.20*
	War Bonus again increased from £93 to £113 as from 1.4.20 then a further advance to £119 as from 1.7.20, got arrears on 3.9.20 £9-6-7
	War allowance increased to £126 as from 1.9.20

5 January 1920	*Birdie and girls gone to Harrison lodging at a farm near, Birdie is to see about work on a small farm she has bought there*
1 May 1920	*Went to see aeroplane starting up on its flight, saw it go up twice and down once*
10 July 1920	*Connie went up in aeroplane 12 minutes price £1.15*
14 December 1920	*Evelyn confined boy*
	1921 Baby christened Theodore Bertram
1 January 1921	*Moved on 1.1.21 from 556 Point Road to Harrison*
20th June 1922	*Sale of Point Road property from Mrs SFA McLeod to Mr J Hunter). Selling price (pounds)£1600. Natal Building Society AND William Palmer & Son (Conveyancing, Trust and General Agency*
4 August 1923	*Leytonstone farm at Harrison. Price as a going concern £1800. A man came to see, said far too dear*
February 1924	*About 1.2.24 Bought a farm for Hector near the Hammarsdale Station between Inchanga station and the Cato Ridge Booth junction line. Price about £1500 as a going concern 190 acres*
30 June 1924	*Harrison, left there on 30.6.24 came to Hammarsdale*
20 November 1924	*Evelyn confined boy*
19 January 1929	*Vera went up in aeroplane on this date. Cost £1.00 time 15 minutes*
19 January 1929 (same date as aeroplane entry above)	*Frank Lloyd married Vera*

3 February 1933	*Felicity Vera and Frank's daughter born*
25 December 1933	*Several similar entries on the same day . . .*
	Recorded under 'K'
	Kiss remember well 20 years ago best ever had
	Recorded under 'L"
	Lovely kiss had 20 years ago this date
	Three penny bit out of pudding keep for luck
16 March 1935	*Vera confined a boy this time name Michael*
8 August 1937	*Florence passed away*
26 August 1939	*Fred my brother passed away fully away on 26 August 1939 in his 88 year*

<u>Later entries (writing gets shaky)</u>

17 June 1940	*Fathers old clock going again glad*
13 July 1940	*Hair cut by Vera*
26 September 1940	*Sheila married to Mr Hall*
24 June 1941	**Herbert died**

3. Prof Herbert MacLeod and his McLeod Gauge

Prof Herbert McLeod LLD, FRS 1841 – 1923

Herbert McLeod, son of Bentley and Louisa Cristall, was first cousin to Herbert McLeod, 'Herbie', the son of George More McLeod and Ellen Cristall. The families are well known to us through the letters Ellen wrote to her sister Louisa about their life as settlers in South Africa, but the Herbert who lived in England was far more widely known especially by the scientific community.

This Herbert was born in 1841 and studied chemistry after he had left school. At the age of nineteen he became assistant chemist in the School of Mines, was engaged in research and contributed papers to the Physical, Chemical and Royal societies. At the age of thirty he was appointed Professor of Chemistry at the newly established Civil Engineering College at Cooper's Hill and remained in that post for thirty years.

He became a Fellow of the Royal Society in 1881. He was made an Honorary Graduate, LLD of St Andrews University in1907.

The most widely known of his inventions was the McLeod Vacuum Gauge, which remained in use into the 1950s at least. It was used for measuring low pressure gases, and was widely used in industry. It was operated by mercury and was superseded by electrical gauges.

Prof McLeod was a popular lecturer and teacher and his lectures were well illustrated by experiments, and he was sound, accurate and well informed. He was also a humble man in that he did not boast or speak about his achievements. Also he was a deeply spiritual person.

By pure chance Constance MacLeod met Jim Warren, who had worked with a McLeod Gauge locally, and he was delighted to discover a relative who knew about it. He arranged in 1984 for her to visit the factory where he had used the gauge.

1984 Constance MacLeod being shown a McLeod Gauge

www.ingramcontent.com/pod-product-compliance
Lightning Source LLC
Chambersburg PA
CBHW070555300426
44113CB00010B/1263